The Soviet West

edited by
Ralph S. Clem
foreword by
Edward Allworth

 Published in cooperation with the
Program on Soviet Nationality Problems,
Graduate Seminar Research Series,
Columbia University

The Praeger Special Studies program—
utilizing the most modern and efficient book
production techniques and a selective
worldwide distribution network—makes
available to the academic, government, and
business communities significant, timely
research in U.S. and international economic, social, and political development.

The Soviet West
Interplay between Nationality and Social Organization

PRAEGER SPECIAL STUDIES IN INTERNATIONAL POLITICS AND GOVERNMENT

37051

Praeger Publishers   New York   Washington   London

Library of Congress Cataloging in Publication Data

Main entry under title:

The Soviet West.

(Praeger special studies in international politics and
government)
"Published in cooperation with the Program on Soviet
Nationality Problems, Graduate Seminar Research Series,
Columbia University. "
Bibliography: p.
1. Minorities—Russia. 2. Nationalism and socialism.
3. Federal government—Russia. I. Clem, Ralph S. , ed.'
JN6520. M5S656   323. 1'47   74-14040
ISBN 0-275-09840-0

PRAEGER PUBLISHERS
111 Fourth Avenue, New York, N.Y. 10003, U.S.A.
5, Cromwell Place, London SW7 2JL, England

Published in the United States of America in 1975
by Praeger Publishers, Inc.

Printed in the United States of America

The nationality question is regional in scope and essence. Ordinarily the question is thought to involve either a lone self-conscious ethnic group in isolation or a whole state, but nothing midway between or overlapping the two of them. The intermediate possibilities are largely ignored. Although studies of the two extremes produce considerable information, they generate surprisingly few significant insights into the basic aspects of the nationality question or its workings within a particular region.

In the territory under the Soviet regime, more than under its Czarist predecessor, there has been a tendency to view the nationality question as a symmetrical array of separate interrelations somehow external to each ethnic group but linking the Russians (the ruling circle) separately with every single nationality. The question, in reality, is much more complex, for nationalities have persistent internal vitality of their own. It is nourished by many forces including everyday domestic life, the interplay between a nationality and its local milieu, and the connection among close or related neighbors. These have perhaps even more to do with maintaining and vitalizing community and with ethnic contentment or discontent than do decrees, regulations, and policy statements issuing from afar. In the Soviet case, the main population concentrations of most non-Russian regions comprising the USSR lie a fair distance from the Soviet capital located in the Russian Soviet Federated Socialist Republic. This remoteness appears to accent the ethnic insularity of the various nationality regions.

Because the nationality question is a matter of the fundamental satisfaction or dissatisfaction of a nationality in its immediate and extended environment, the process every nationality undergoes in adjusting to the facts of its group life reflects the status of that question in the given zone. This process of accommodation is often obscure, and the pertinent facts are always innumerable. That is one reason why simultaneously analyzing the entire range of problems making up the nationality question in a very large combination of such zones probably is impractical if not impossible, especially if the analyst cannot spend long periods freely circulating and examining data in the countries being studied.

Understanding the workings of the nationality question therefore comes naturally through scrutinizing the balance between satisfaction or dissatisfaction evidenced within a nationality's full environment (zone) or in a manageable set of zones making up a distinct region.

v

A zone is defined by the nationality's own views, distribution, and pertinent linkages to other groups, so that actual zonal limits may or may not correspond to administrative, topographical, or other units often thought to identify a nationality's area. When a set of such zones is considered in studying nationality problems, the pattern and totality of the findings are usually more important than discoveries about individual groups in revealing the crux of the nationality question.

Not just any collection of nationality zones offers promising results to the scholar investigating the nationality question. A suitable region usually either bears a recognized designation or has been marked off in human activity by a combination of attitudes and economic, administrative, cultural or other boundaries. If nationality regions encompassing a number of zones seldom quickly accept the names attached to them by outsiders, in time they sometimes adopt them for at least some purposes. "Central Asia" provides one example in which a name, handy for outsiders, long remained virtually meaningless locally, but slowly has come into currency in the area to some extent. When such a thing happens, the symbolism of the designation applied very likely relates to far more than the terrain or location distinguishing the particular region.

Because of Russia's huge breadth, Russian policy-makers have regarded the Czarist Empire up to 1917 as well as its successor, the present Union of Soviet Socialist Republics, as a power entitled through geographical position to prerogatives in both Europe and Asia. This emphasis upon the intercontinental span of the USSR has been reinforced recently in the East by tensions rising along the common frontier dividing the People's Republic of China from the Soviet Union, as well as by the sharp competition between those two major Communist countries concerning which of them should exert primary influence throughout Asia.

Thus, Soviet scholars, following Czarist precedent, have repeatedly recognized in print the appropriateness of terminology like "Russian Far East," "Asiatic Russia," or "Soviet Asia." But among the acknowledged regions of this kind comprising the USSR, a curious analogic gap, perhaps not troublesome during Czarist times, leaps at once to the mind of anyone contemplating the Soviet Union today. Far from the eastern limits of the Soviet expanse lies a substantial strip of territory sandwiched between a portion of the Russian Soviet Federated Socialist Republic which Soviet books commonly refer to as "European Russia" and East Central Europe (Poland, Czechoslovakia, Hungary and Romania). While that Soviet frontier area helps screen Russia proper from the outside world, it intimately contacts Europe from Scandinavia to the lower Danube. Yet the area has remained without a unifying designation, though clearly the westernmost

vi

reach of the USSR. Probably this omission on the authorities' part stems from an inhibition acquired with an Imperial Russian mentality dominated by the thought that much of that strip, including the Ukraine (formerly "Little Russia" to some) was part of old Russia, as was some of Finland, Moldavia, Poland, and what is now Belorussia. In addition, Moscow, Leningrad and their environs appear to represent a "European Russia" determined to secure an aura of Europeanness ("westernness," modernity) long desired. This distinction may be wanted to help justify the practice of attaching the appellation "advanced" to Russkii narod (Russian people) but not to names of any Soviet nationalities, no matter how civilized.

W hatever the internal explanation for avoiding the idea of a "West" analogous to the frequently mentioned Soviet "East," the authors of the present book have made a persuasive case for treating as a unit the region embracing the constituent USSR republics this side of Russia. Ralph S. Clem and his colleagues have shown clearly in these chapters not only that the USSR's westernmost region is the "Soviet West" by virtue of more than compass readings, but that concentrating research upon such an area yields insights into the nationality question hardly accessible through different means.

One basic pattern carefully researched in the present volume encompasses the interplay on the one hand between efforts by the authorities in the region to promote increasing social homogeneity within each nationality and on the other hand the response or reaction of the nationality to those efforts. Knowledge concerning the entirety of this interplay in the chosen set of nationality zones becomes a valuable aid in comprehending the nationality question throughout that region, and, by extension, in the Soviet Union at large. The present study and a previous work, The Nationality Question in Soviet Central Asia (1973), both based in good part on research conducted by the interdisciplinary graduate Seminar in Soviet Nationality Problems, Columbia University, have taken the regional approach to analysis of the nationality question, and both have posted interesting results.

Though the Soviet West differs from Central Asia in nearly every pertinent respect, this pair of investigations shows that the balance of satisfaction and dissatisfaction within each of the two regions in the early 1970s contrasts even more strikingly than local conditions. Despite a range of technological disabilities generally conceded, Central Asian self-confidence and satisfaction seem to be vigorously on the rise, whereas acknowledged Soviet Western advantages and impressive development have recently failed to sustain either general self-assurance or contentment in the region. This crucial variation relates to imagined or perceived deprivation, recent and present achievements, to expectations, to fair treatment from neighbors or higher authorities, processes of urbanization, and other,

vii

especially internal, factors. These finding relating to the Soviet West are also corroborated by others reached in an unpublished inquiry concerning the Transcaucasus completed during 1970-1971 by the same Seminar, whose participants then concluded that regional life, relations, and their history, were of primary, not secondary, importance in the workings of the nationality question there.

In this study of the Soviet West the emphasis has deliberately been placed upon the region's internal developments rather than on policies initiated outside this set of nationality zones. Besides exposing regional patterns, the work reveals much about affairs in each component nationality zone, and each chapter supplies quantities of information or interpretations new to the field. In several instances, the authors also provide a concise historical background useful in understanding contemporary nationality affairs. Among the most unusual, needed chapters in the compilation are two pertaining to the Moldavian Soviet Socialist Republic. The bibliography appended at the end of this volume makes obvious the scarcity of materials in English concerning today's Soviet Moldavia. Here, both Nicholas Dima and Walter Feldman employ contemporary Moldavian-language sources extensively. Map 2, showing the intricacies of the Moldavian situation, also helps greatly to convey the interpenetration between Europe and the Soviet West which influences the latter so strongly.

Taken as a whole, no other published interdisciplinary work of this kind that comes to mind more nearly achieves the goal of focusing systematically and effectively upon a defined and multinational Soviet region for the purpose of illuminating the nature of the Soviet nationality question in general.

The chapters in this volume are derived from papers written
for the graduate Seminar in Soviet Nationality Problems, Columbia
University, during 1972-73. The authors collectively extend their
appreciation to Professors Edward Allworth and Robert Austerlitz
of Columbia University for their most valuable comments and suggestions regarding the formulation of the topics and investigation of
the problems. The editor is indebted to Professor Allworth for his
considerable contribution to the finalization of the seminar papers.

These papers were presented at the Open Seminar on Nationality
Problems in the Soviet West, held at Columbia University on May
5, 1973. The authors gained much from critiques of these papers
by Professors Frederick C. Barghoorn of Yale University and Yaroslav Bilinsky of the University of Delaware.

Also, the editor expresses his thanks to Christopher Brest of
the Department of Geography, Columbia University, for drawing the
maps, and to Amy Davey of the Bureau of Applied Social Research,
for typing the manuscript.

The Open Conference on Nationality Problems in the Soviet
West was sponsored by the Program on Soviet Nationality Problems,
Columbia University (Edward Allworth, Director). In addition, the
Program financed the cartography, typing, and other administrative
support for the compilation of this volume.

When the conceptual framework of the seminar was formulated,
the term "nationality vitality" was adopted as an expression of the
persistent quality of ethnicity. Subsequently, we adopted other phrases
with like meanings to avoid the repetition of this one expression with
its rhyming syllables throughout the text. Yet, no other phrasing
seems to carry the message as well as the original, the message
that nationality is not merely a neutral trait which endures, but
rather can be a positive force that shapes and influences society.
We ask the reader, therefore, to bear this critical distinction in
mind.

Two technical points are in order. The transliteration system
utilized in this volume is that specified in Edward Allworth's Nationalities of the Soviet East: Publications and Writing Systems (New
York: Columbia University Press, 1971). Finally, the use of the
term "nationalities" throughout this work excludes the Russians,
whereas "ethnic groups" includes both the nationalities and the
Russians.

CONTENTS

x

37051

LIST OF FIGURES, MAPS, AND TABLE

Figures

Maps

Table

The Soviet West

THE SOVIET WEST: 1970

FINLAND
HELSINKI

LENINGRAD

BALTIC
SEA

TALLIN
ESTONIAN
SSR

RSFSR

RIGA LATVIAN
SSR

LITHUANIAN
SSR

MOSCOW

KAUNAS
VILNIUS

RSFSR

MINSK

BELORUSSIAN
SSR

POLAND

KIEV

L'VOV

UKRAINIAN   SSR

KHAR'KOV

CZECH.

HUNG.

DONETSK

ROMANIA

MOLDAVIAN
SSR

KISHINEV

ODESSA

SEA OF
AZOV

BLACK SEA

REPUBLIC BOUNDARY
INTERNATIONAL
         BOUNDARY
★ REPUBLIC CAPITAL
○ OTHER CITIES
0   100   200 Miles
0   100   200   300 Kilometers

1

**VITALITY OF THE
NATIONALITIES IN
THE SOVIET WEST:
BACKGROUND AND
IMPLICATIONS**
Ralph S. Clem

During the summer of 1972, a dramatic chain of events occurred in the Soviet republic of Lithuania. Two youths committed suicide by self-immolation. Street fighting involved thousands of young people with police and paratroops, and many civilians were detained.[1] During that same year, Soviet authorities revealed that they had arrested a number of important Ukrainians, intellectuals who were alleged to have conducted an extensive underground nationalist movement that issued clandestine publications, and which supposedly had ties to anti-Communist emigre groups.[2] In 1971, officials of the Latvian Communist party apparently had felt constrained by events to caution Latvians against expressing overt anti-Russian sentiments.[3]

These occurrences, and others perhaps more subtle and more significant, are characteristic of trends that have in large measure prompted an increase in attention to the importance of and interest in problems associated with nationality in the Soviet Union. Among all the regions of the USSR, open anti-Soviet dissent appears to be, as the above events tend to confirm, most intense in the Soviet West.* These events are symptomatic, in the Soviet context, of the fundamental stresses arising from the contradictory forces of nationality consciousness on the one hand, and strong pressures for homogenization on the other, at work in the USSR.

---

*The Soviet West is defined, for present purposes, as consisting of the Soviet Republics of Estonia, Latvia, Lithuania, Belorussia, the Ukraine, and Moldavia. The Autonomous Republic of Karelia was omitted only because the source materials (local press) required for this detailed inquiry were not available at the time this work was begun.

The aim of this coordinated inquiry is to cast light upon aspects of the nationality question (the role and importance of nationality), hopefully illuminating the crucial interface between nationality consciousness and the pressures for homogenization.[4] Developed to help accomplish this goal were a set of working premises common to each individual research effort, a common methodology and consistent exploitation of sources, and a sketch of some broad implications to be drawn from the interdisciplinary study of the nationality question.

The chapters in this volume cover a wide range of topics and investigate the interaction between nationality and other forces within sectors of society in the Soviet West on three broad levels: cultural, socioeconomic, and political. The cultural realm, including language and literature, is a critical area with regard to nationality identity; this is as true in the Soviet West as in most multiethnic settings. Three chapters treat this important topic with special reference to Soviet attempts to utilize the cultural and linguistic realm as a means of influencing ethnic distinctiveness. In one instance (Estonia), the government and Party exert homogenizing forces upon language and literature; the forces taking shape as directives from administrative bodies and as criticism in the media. Interestingly, Soviet authorities strive to employ the same channels and forces to reinforce the distinctiveness of another nationality (Moldavia) in an apparent effort to combat irredentism.

In any modernizing multinational state, definite tensions exist between integrative forces dictated by economic considerations and the centrifugal tendencies characteristic of an ethnically based federation. These opposing forces within socioeconomic sectors of the Soviet West are examined with reference to the modernized segments of society in the Ukraine, the economic management system of Latvia, and the educational and technical training institutions in Lithuania. Essentially, although strong pressures for integration are constantly in evidence, and despite substantial economic inducements, the nationalities of the Soviet West continue to display nationality assertiveness in the socioeconomic sectors.

The last broad topic under consideration in this volume concerns the Soviet leadership's widely recognized employment of political organizations as a means of influencing various groups. Attention in the final three chapters focuses upon the interaction between nationality and the political sectors, specifically the Party, Komsomol, and the military-patriotic organization (DOSAAF) in Belorussia, Lithuania, and Estonia, respectively. The scope of cultural, socioeconomic, and political sectors analyzed in the nine chapters that follow, taken together with the variety of geographic, economic, and historical features of the Soviet West as an entity, provides the basis for an understanding of nationality perseverance in the area.

2

The Soviet West, a region extending through an arc from the
Gulf of Finland in the north to the Black Sea in the south, is an area
with enough important characteristics common to its major consti-
tuents to be considered as an entity, yet with sufficient diversity to
provide interesting and significant comparisons. The most important
single factor common to all units of the Soviet West is, of course,
that they are not Russian. Historically, the nationalities of the Soviet
West have ties with other, non-Soviet countries, ties which are to
varying degrees maintained to this day. These links, whether cultural,
linguistic, or religious, lend to the region a unique character. The
Soviet West is "western" in two meanings: in the obvious connotation
as the western region of the Soviet Union, and more important, as
that region of the USSR which has the strongest identification with
Europe. Estonians share linguistic and some cultural traits with
Finland; Lithuania historically has ties with Poland, as does the
Western Ukraine; and Moldavia can be considered as virtually a
Romanian province. Finally, the titular nationalities of the Soviet
West remain mainly unmixed, unlike some other regions of the USSR,
such as Central Asia. With but two exceptions within the Soviet West,
over ninety-seven percent of each republic's titular nationality is
found within its own unit. The exceptions are the Belorussians,
ninety-three percent of whom live in Belorussia, and the Moldavians,
eighty-nine percent of whom live in Moldavia and an additional ten
percent in the contiguous Ukrainian SSR.[5]
The Soviet West is characterized by high to moderate levels
of economic development with relation to other areas of the USSR,
although there are some exceptions to this generalization (Moldavia
and some areas of Belorussia, Lithuania, and the Ukraine remain
comparatively underdeveloped). Within the region, the Baltic republics specialize principally in light and diversified industries (such
as machine-building and appliances); however, the introduction of
natural gas and petroleum pipelines heralds the development of a
substantial chemical industry in this area.[6] Belorussia has undergone significant industrial development within the last decade, as
illustrated by the fact that no Soviet city of over 500,000 increased
in size between 1959 and 1970 by a percentage as high as its capital,
Minsk (only one capital city of a Union republic, Frunze, exceeded
Minsk in percentage increase).[7] The Ukraine is one of the major
areas of extractive and heavy industry in the Soviet Union, with the
greatest concentration of economic activity located in the Eastern
Ukraine around the Donets coal basin. Only Moldavia is predominantly
an agricultural area, although agriculture and food processing remain
very important sectors of the economies of all republics of the Soviet
West. Thus, the Soviet West is an important region of the USSR,
making a contribution to the Soviet economy greater than its share

3

of either the population of the country (27.6 percent) or the area of
the country (4.6 percent).

With important qualifications in the historical and political
sense, there is also a general similarity among republics of the
Soviet West. Four of the units (Estonia, Latvia, Lithuania, and the
Ukraine) have been independent for at least a short time within the
last half-century; Moldavia and Belorussia were not in themselves
independent. Historically, four areas of the Soviet West (Moldavia,
parts of Lithuania, the Western Ukraine, and western Belorussia)
within the recent past comprised parts of other countries. Thus,
annexation into the USSR for a significant portion of the Soviet West
is a post-World War II phenomenon, although the majority of these
territories had at one time or another been part of the Russian Empire under the Czars.

Demographically, the Soviet West is a region of low fertility
and mortality (hence low natural increase). In 1970, only Moldavia
had a natural increase rate above the Union-wide average; Estonia
and Latvia ranked lowest among all republics in natural increase.[8]
A slight majority of the total population of the Soviet West is urban.
Belorussia, Moldavia, Lithuania, and the Ukraine fall below the Soviet
average of fifty-six percent urban, while Estonia and Latvia rank
numbers one and three respectively among all republics of the USSR
in the level of urbanization.[9] With regard to educational standing,
people of the Ukraine, Latvia, and Estonia rose above the Union-wide
average of those over ten years of age having secondary education
and higher. Moldavia, Lithuania, and Belorussia were below average.[10]
Thus, although fertility, mortality, and natural increase are almost
universally low in the Soviet West, there are significant disparities
in the socioeconomic levels, running roughly along a gradient from
high in the north to low in the south. (See Data Appendix II.)

The greatest heterogeneity among republics and nationalities
of the Soviet West is evident in the cultural realm. Of the six major
titular nationalities, all have significantly different languages (although Ukrainian and Belorussian, and Latvian and Lithuanian are
related), and religion ranges from Lutheran (Estonians, Latvians)
through Roman Catholic (Lithuanians) to Orthodox (Belorussians,
Ukrainians, Moldavians), with some groups (Belorussians and Ukrainians) having more than one major sectarian affiliation. These, and
other, cultural differences have in the past exerted divisive influences
on supra-national affiliations.

The interdependent premises providing the bases for the individual research efforts comprising this volume include the following: (1) The economic and cultural situation which prevails in the
Soviet West makes the nationalities of the region subject to intensive
pressures for integration and homogenization with one another;

4

(2) despite this fact, and perhaps partly because of it (because of a local sense of vulnerability to such integrative pressures), nationality asserts its divisiveness and vitality in the region today. By "pressures" are meant those efforts exerted by supranationality or area-wide administrative organizations, social mobilization and modernization efforts (including higher educational levels, increased urbanization, participation in non-agricultural occupations, and the like), and other influences. "Vitality" is used here to refer to the retention and perpetuation of effective nationality identity by individual ethnic groups in the Soviet West. Thus, it is contended that two sets of forces are operating (those forces relating to efforts for homogenization, and those forces deriving from nationality consciousness), usually in opposition, within various sectors of society in the Soviet West.

Against this very general background the methodology utilized in each individual chapter has entailed the application of the working premises adopted by the entire interdisciplinary group. The group defined the general arena of inquiry and noted that the interaction of nationalities within identifiable sectors of society would provide the focus of attention. Therefore, the research group insured that each republic of the Soviet West would be treated and, within each republic, selected some cultural, socioeconomic, or political body as a focus. These sectors of society were defined either along organizational lines (the Party, Komsomol, Red Army), in the functional sense (the educational system, economic management), in some instances by demographic criteria (the modernized sector, youth), or by other means (literary, intellectual, and linguistic fields). Some sectors may be more clearly distinguishable than others, but the common methodology remains the same regardless of the nature of the sector, and can be summarized as follows:

(1) Define the sector to be examined.

(2) Describe the nature of integrative and divisive forces at work within the sector.

(3) Assess the implications of nationality interaction with the sector of society and the nature of integrative and divisive forces within the sector for the total nationality consciousness or homogenization.

(4) Relate pertinent aspects of this interplay between nationality and social organizations not only to the individual republics but to the Soviet West in general.

In addition to adopting the common methodological approach, each author searched the local Soviet press of the appropriate republic for evidence of nationality interaction within the specified sector. The scope of this survey of the local Soviet press generally was purposely concentrated within the period 1970-1973. The nature of the evidence sought in the local press and its evaluation naturally depended upon the sector examined; each contributor offers remarks about the evidence sought, the evidence found, and gives interpretations thereof. Whenever feasible, sources in the language of the nationality under investigation were utilized; otherwise, the Russian-language press of the republic in question was surveyed. Specifically, local-language sources were exploited for those inquiries concerning Estonia, Moldavia, and the Ukraine.

Although the topics under investigation were diverse, the common conclusion was that, without exception, nationality remains an important and vital force in the Soviet West within sectors of society on all levels. Thus, the Party continues to confront nationality consciousness within the framework of the federal structure, nationality integration into modernized society remains a question of major importance, indigenous and homogenizing forces oppose one another in the literary and linguistic fields, and issues of competing nationality identities warrant constant attention. Moreover, the role and importance of nationality and the pressures for homogenization are evident in the schools, in the factory management, among the youth, and in the military.

The chapters in this volume are organized in a progression from those concerned with cultural sectors, to those investigating socioeconomic sectors, and finally to those relating to political organizations; each of these broad categories consists of three chapters. It is hoped that by focusing on the Soviet West as an important arena for study, by the application of specialized methodology in common, and by utilizing extensively what may be called parallel sources from the Soviet press, a clearer understanding of the pressures for and against integration or persistence of nationality consciousness in this pivotal area may have been reached.

NOTES

1. "200 Lithuanians Reported Jailed," New York Times, June 14, 1972, p. 1.

2. Theodore Shabad, "Soviet Discloses Ukraine Unrest," New York Times, June 7, 1972, p. 7.

3. "Latvians Chided for Nationalism," New York Times, March 21, 1971, p. 17.

4. See Edward Allworth, "Restating the Soviet Nationality Question," in Soviet Nationality Problems, ed. Edward Allworth (New York: Columbia University Press, 1971), pp. 1-21.

5. Itogi vsesoiuznoi perepisi naseleniia 1970 goda (Moscow: Statistika, 1973), IV, pp. 321-30.

6. Theodore Shabad, Basic Industrial Resources of the U.S.S.R. (New York: Columbia University Press, 1969), pp. 201-06.

7. Narodnoe khoziaistvo SSSR v 1969 g. (Moscow: Statistika, 1970), pp. 23-28.

8. Narodnoe khoziaistvo SSSR v 1970 g. (Moscow: Statistika, 1971), pp. 50-51.

9. Ibid., pp. 10-11.

10. Ibid., p. 25.

2

**LANGUAGE AND
LITERATURE IN
ESTONIA:
KULTURPOLITIK OR
NATURAL EVOLUTION?**
Joan T. Weingard

Despite a continuous flow of directives from the Estonian Ministry of Culture and Communist party (often as an intermediary for the
central government) and from the central government and Party
directly that urge the adoption of the principles of socialist realism
in art and criticism, some Estonians involved in the verbal arts and
related fields (stylistics, normative linguistics and language modernization, and literary criticism) reflect or perpetuate nationality consciousness in both the content and form of their works.

This hypothesis will be employed to throw light on three aspects
of the problem of the expression of nationality consciousness in the
above-mentioned fields: language, cultural history, and the current,
ongoing literary production, regarding them as a hierarchy of prerequisites in which the lack of any one renders the implementation
of the following one impractical, if not impossible. The principal
source utilized is Sirp ja Vasar (Sickle and Hammer), the weekly
publication of the Ministry of Culture and Writers, Artists, and Composers unions of Estonia from November 1972 to March 1973. This
publication offers a richer source of material concerning language
and literature than the daily press, while having a sufficiently large
circulation (over 20,000) at least by Estonian standards, to be considered more than a journal for a limited audience of specialists.
Keel ja Kirjandus (Language and Literature), for example, has a
monthly edition of barely over 3,000 copies, a significant proportion
of which is probably sent abroad. Daily and monthly sources have
also been surveyed: Rahva Hääl (The People's Voice) for September
and October 1972, and January 1973, and Looming (Art) for June and
July 1972.

In effect, I will be dealing with the quadrilateral relationship
shown in Figure 1,

FIGURE 1

Relationship of Language, Literature, and Nationality in Estonia

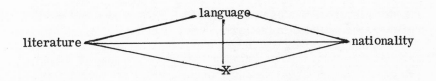

in which X refers to the sum of the cultural implications of the social, political, and economic system of the Soviet Union. There is apparently no body of accepted definitions and terminology dealing with all four of these variables simultaneously, and it is therefore necessary to mention in advance certain types of distinctions that have emerged from the data and that can be seen as serving as a framework for it. These are provisional distinctions which may be applicable only to the time, place, and situation in question, and should not be construed as an attempt to establish a metatheory for this type of set of inter-relationships.

A distinction between form and content with regard to literature must be observed. The first refers to purely linguistic questions and the second to subject matter and its treatment. This is vaguely similar but not entirely congruent with the terms in the slogan "National in form, socialist in content," with which, however, it should not be confused. In the domain of language, a distinction between internal and external (with respect to the nationality) orientation of usage prevails. This refers to the fact that the nationality language is used practically exclusively for intranationality communication while another tongue must be used for extranationality purposes.

Specifically regarding pressure for integration, there is a distinction between Russification and Sovietization. There is also a distinction between overt and covert which reflects the difference between official statements and directives on one hand, and practices or tendencies that have a very real effect but no identifiable source on the other. Concerning nationality consciousness, there is an active/passive distinction, of which the first refers to current productive activities and the second to the accessibility and exploitability of past linguistic and literary production. There tends to be a coincidence of overt pressure for Sovietization with active response, and covert pressure for Russification with passive response, but this is not a logical or practical necessity.

9

Estonian cultural vitality will be dealt with as a progression from form to content and from passive to active. First, we will consider the dynamics of the current language situation, then the question of the availability of the raw material for a nationality literature, and finally the question of whether the first two elements are in fact being used as the foundation of a distinctively Estonian literature (at which level the problem of integrative pressure by way of socialist realism as mentioned in the hypothesis comes into play).

Although the connection between nationality and language is not absolute, involving the qualification that a certain body of literature can be national in a sense without linguistic distinctiveness,[1] it is the case in Soviet Estonia that language, literature, and nationality have a strong connection. It is therefore advisable to establish the groundlines of the linguistic background of Estonia. Estonian is a Uralic language and one of the three members of this family to achieve the status of a culture language, the other two being Finnish and Hungarian. It should be borne in mind that in a language family so sparsely represented on the world scene, abstract knowledge of linguistic relationship may transcend such mundane considerations as mutual intelligibility.

The first concrete evidence of Estonian as a language of publication appears in the early 1500s, at which time the output consisted of translated religious works. A genuine Estonian literature, secular and not translated from German, did not reach significant proportions until the nineteenth century, when it was closely allied with the awakening of nationality awareness.[2] Although Estonia was incorporated within Russia at the time, the pervasively dominant foreign element in the literature was German. With regard to the actual structure of standard Estonian, both grammar and vocabulary have submitted to many changes in the twentieth century.[3]

LANGUAGE ROLES IN ESTONIA

The picture of language roles and uses in Soviet Estonia is fairly complex. Combining the concept of the sociologically complete language with the internal/external distinction discussed above, the following model of Estonian language roles can be formed (Figure 2).

Russian as an internal complete language refers, strictly speaking, to knowledge of Russian by Estonians and their use of it in situations which require it. It does not directly refer to the use of Russian by Russians who are residents of the Republic but not members of the Estonian nationality. It should be noted, however, that as the proportion of Russians in Estonia increases, the number of potential situations that might demand the use of Russian on the part of an Estonian will likewise increase.

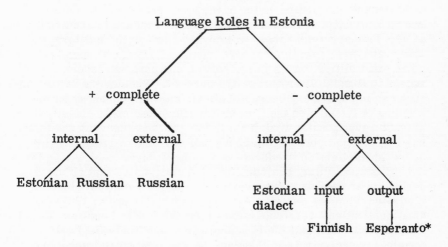

FIGURE 2

Language Roles in Estonia

*This slot could be occupied by any politically neutral language. Esperanto was chosen in part because it epitomizes the absence of political affiliations.

Even such a situation as simple bilingualism is rarely stable, so it is not unreasonable to expect that the Estonian language-role picture is a likely field in which to look for signs of development with relevance to the nationality question. The two extremes to which one could imagine the "tree" being bent are depicted in Figures 3 and 4.

Official pronouncement tends to concern itself with the left side of the tree shown in Figures 2, 3, and 4 (Russian and the nationality language). The Communist party of the Soviet Union, in a pronouncement that was included in preparations for the fifty-year jubilee of the founding of the USSR, stated that while the development of written languages for all nationalities and nationality groups is a part of official policy, all nationalities and nationality groups of the USSR have freely chosen Russian as a common language of inter-nationality relations and cooperation.[4] Thus, on the most idealistic level, Russian is seen as confined to external use in relation to nationality populations. There are, however, three roles of Russian which emerge from the Estonian press: as a transmitter language (external output), as a replacement language, and as a model language (external input). One of the few articles in the Estonian daily press that dealt specifically with the language situation reflected the first two roles. Under the title "The Russian Language in my Life" were included six essays by Estonians expounding on the advantages and joys to be derived from a knowledge of Russian and urging the readers to acquire the same. Primary among these are advancement in the military, the Party, and other prestige careers; communication with members of other nationalities, on both professional and personal levels; and access to Russian literature in the original. Whether the article as such has in reality any degree of effectiveness in encouraging the learning of Russian on the part of Estonians (one could classify it as at least a functionally weak form of integrative pressure), the testimony of the contributors, which we will examine in greater detail below, sheds light on two facets of language roles.

First, V. Vilks, chairman of a kolhhoz, stated that although during his student days (presumably in the early sixties, since he graduated from the Estonian Academy of Agriculture in 1965) technical publications were cultivated in the nationality language alongside Russian, now over half the technical literature in his field (dairy farming) is exclusively in Russian. Second, there are interesting undulations that can be observed concerning the study of Russian and Estonian in the school system. L. Lebbin, a language course director from Tallin, refers to the learning "with care and fondness" of Estonian by Russians living in Tallin that has "noticeably increased" in recent years. How much of this is simply "velvet glove" is, of course, debatable, but it may be taken to indicate that some slight but not insignificant degree of Estonianization of Russian immigrants has been continuing in Soviet times. The other side of the educational

FIGURE 3

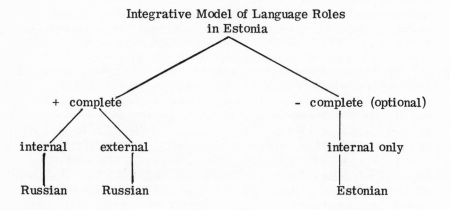

Integrative Model of Language Roles
in Estonia

FIGURE 4

Nationality Vitality Model of Language Roles
in Estonia

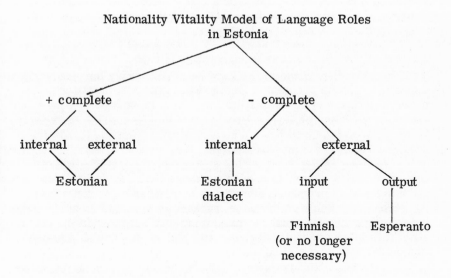

coin is given by U. Buschmann, director of a Tallin middle school,
who refers to the problem of Estonian students neglecting their study
of Russian and speculates about its cause.[5]

A more widely publicized facet is the role of Russian as a dis-
seminator of Estonian literary endeavor. Estonia is a very small
nation and not unaware of its insignificance in the eyes of the world,
in view not only of the small number of ethnic Estonians but also of
the virtual nonexistence of foreigners interested in appreciating
Estonian literature in the original. It is, therefore, not surprising
to find many articles in Sirp ja Vasar, especially in the jubilee year,
dealing with the advantages to Estonia of belonging to the Soviet Union
with regard to the translation and dissemination of Estonian literary
works in Russian and the nationality languages.

T. Velliste mentions the exhibitions of Soviet Estonian literature
held in the RSFSR, the German Democratic Republic, Czechoslovakia,
Canada, Sweden (perhaps particularly significant as an emigre center)
and Finland.[6] J. Kabin compares the quantity of Estonian literature
in translation during the period of independence (199 works for a total
of 600,000 copies) with that of the period from 1940 to 1971 (460 works
into Russian alone for a total of 20 million copies and 250 into other
nationality languages for a total of 3.5 million copies).[7] Püss and
Miller, along similar lines, note that Estonian literature has now
been translated, besides Russian, into 20 Soviet languages, among
which Latvian and Ukrainian figure numerically most prominently.[8]

One may wonder whether there is any point to the translation and dissemination of Estonian literature if it has lost any distinctively Estonian characteristics in translation, but it is necessary to refrain from discussing this matter until later.

Having considered Russian as a replacement language in at least some functions and as a transmitter language, there remains the third role, that of the model language. Like many languages today, Estonian faces the problem of finding words for new inventions, theoretical entities, and social institutions. This is handled to a large extent on the Republic level. Problems in this field arise in two ways. In the first, which constitutes lexical innovation proper, it can, for example, come to the attention of the Language and Literature Institute of the Academy of Sciences (which supervises the introduction of neologisms) that a word is needed for some object (such as "Cosmetics") and a solution is proposed, sometimes by popular competition. In the second, a specific item (name, passage of text, and so on) presenting certain problems must be translated from Russian. In the latter case, it is more accurate, perhaps, to speak of Russian as a translation model than as a lexical donor.

The role of Russian with regard to the first aspect of the model language role is negligible, despite the statements of H. Meriste, member of the translation department of the Journalists' Union, whose avowals of Estonian lexical indebtedness to Russian are completely at variance with the data he presents.[9] Although Slavic loanwords have been entering Estonian for a long time, the number of loanwords borrowed directly from Russian and of Russian origin since the beginning of the Soviet period has been surprisingly low: a handful of terms closely related to the system such as sovhooz, kolhooz, krai, and rajoon are among the few that have a large statistical frequency in the current journalistic language. Judging from Meriste's data and the journalistic language that one encounters in the local press, Estonian draws on three sources for loanwords: (1) So-called "international" words (possibly through the Russian language but not in themselves distinctively Russian) like sotsialism, buldooser, skreeper; (2) Adoption of dialect terms into the standard language with specialized meaning: tuusik, now "voucher for accommodations"; (3) Calquing, in which subdivision according to model language follows semantic fields. Some calques, referring to Soviet institutions, are formed from Russian. For example, the expression "Five-Year Plan" is formed:

viis—aasta—k (Estonian)
piati—let—ka (Russian)

Those of other semantic fields may frequently follow a Finnish model.

The second type of Russian influence, as a translation model, is not part of an official language policy on any level and is therefore easiest to illustrate by reaction against it. A letter from a militia major refers with pleasure and gratitude to U. Liivak's book Where the Shoe Pinches the Language (which deals with problems occasioned by the use of Russian as a translation model), saying that he comes into daily contact with official and judicial materials translated word-for-word from Russian and mentioning a "dragon of a sentence bristling with Russicisms and thought-inflation."[10] Meriste, in discussing problems of translation, mentions the fact that the Estonian name for the new journalism building in Tallin was to be chosen as a translation of a Russian name which was originally given to the building.[11] It is inevitable that the vast quantity of written and broadcast Estonian that is obliged to be a direct translation from Russian will have an effect on Estonian syntax and vocabulary. This is not necessarily part of the Estonian nationality question as such as regards overt integrative pressure (model languages other than Russian, even Finnish, are also subject to criticism), but the concern taken by at least some writers about the purity of the language is an indicator of at least a minimum degree of nationality perseverance.

Despite their limitations in speakers and usage, the noncomplete languages play key roles, perhaps more as types than as tokens, in the linguistic mosaic of Soviet Estonia. Finnish is a typical "Big Brother" language, providing an example of how a language with a similar phonological and prosodic structure, as well as a similarly obscure history and status, can cope not only with lexical innovations but also with gaining some degree of international literary recognition. Finnish will be discussed more specifically below when dealing with Balto-Finnic cultural contacts, but let us mention now that Helmuth Kasealu, head of the publishing house Valgus, stated in an interview that the publication of an Estonian-Finnish dictionary was that publishing house's greatest accomplishment of the year.[12]

Esperanto, on the other hand, typifies the neutral transmitter language with no implication of political domination. Although it is almost inconceivable that it will ever become the sole transmitter language of Estonia (and also unlikely that this would be desirable), translation into Esperanto was one of the primary means of dissemination of Estonian literature abroad during the period of independence[13] and interest continues today: an Esperanto news column appears in Keel ja Kirjandus, an Estonian novel was recently translated into Esperanto (E. Krusten's Okupacio [Occupation], 12,000 copies),[14] and the works of some Soviet Estonian authors have appeared in Esperanto publications outside the Soviet Union. If this seems trivial, it should be regarded against the background of government statements that Russian is the choice of all Soviet nationalities as the language of inter-nationality and world communication.

There are also a few instances of expressed discontent with Russian as a transmitter language: in a comment on an article in the Polish publication Magazyn Filmowy about the Estonian film Antarktika Suvel (In the Antarctic Summer) it is regretted that inaccuracies mar the text. Among those cited are the misspelling of proper names: Sjejet for Sööd, Priat for Pärd.15 It is likely that the difficulties with the vowels come from transliteration into and out of Cyrillic, although the metathesis in Priat may be of Polish origin. Of a similar nature is Tuudur Vettik's complaint in his article on Estonian choral music about the mispronunciation of the names of Estonian composers and conductors in the Russian language broadcasts on Estonian radio.16 The same problem in reverse is referred to by Alma Saare in a comment on the misspelling of English names in the serial "Detektiivide sajand" ("Century of the Detectives") in Noorte Hääl (Voice of Youth), blaming it in part on the mediation of Russian.17

The situation regarding the South-Estonian dialect is, if not unique, at least highly unusual in the Soviet Union and perhaps outside it as well. The main cleavage of Estonian dialects is into a northern and a southern group. The literary language of Estonia is based largely on the north Estonian dialects (whether for historical reasons or from some language-internal simplicity metric remains to be investigated), despite the fact that the south of the country has been in a position of economic and cultural primacy. The South-Estonian dialect has persisted, however, not only as a spoken language but also as the language of poetry for some writers from that area to such a degree that Ain Kaalep, in reviewing a book of poetry by a south Estonian poet who is making increasing use of dialect in his verse, suggested that all writers using South-Estonian dialect agree upon an orderly system of spelling for the convenience of the reader.18

Interesting though it be, it is unclear whether there is any significance relevant to nationality questions in this phenomenon. It is unlikely that emphasis on South-Estonian could serve as a wedge for the central government in order to weaken nationality identity. First, it is just as likely that Estonian nationality identity will be strengthened as weakened in response to such tactics and second, it is questionable whether there is any use in fragmenting a nationality already so small. The South-Estonian dialect question is probably best taken as an indication of self-image: there is a lack of stigma not only on the nationality level but on the local level as well. It should also serve as a reminder that despite occasional references to Estonia as a representative of a Western type of "nation-state" entity, the Estonian nationality, while prefigured in nineteenth century literature, was largely thrown together in the first two decades of the twentieth century and had only twenty years of independence to congeal.

Having dealt with the two complete and three noncomplete languages which play a role in Estonia today, one can conclude that integrative pressure is tending to expand the use of Russian as an internal complete language and to retain it as an external complete language, but not explicitly to use it extensively as a model language or a total replacement language for all its speakers in all social contexts. Expression of nationality consciousness is shown through the retention and cultivation of Estonian as an internal complete language wherever possible and through interest in an alternative to Russian as an external language.

THE STATUS OF ESTONIAN CULTURAL HISTORY

So far, we have dealt with the linguistic variables in Estonia that serve as a backdrop for the verbal arts of the Republic. The relatively healthy state of the language is irrelevant if one cannot establish the existence of a contentually distinctive nationality literature. For practical purposes, it is necessary to divide this question into two parts: (1) material showing awareness of their own folk materials and literary history, and (2) production of modern literature with roots in the first.

At the present time, there is little perceptible pressure exerted on Estonians to prevent or distort passive awareness of their national cultural heritage. There is bias in the presentation of history but this does not usually affect evaluations of the works themselves. A tendency in this direction can be seen already in 1966 in an article on the patriotic poetry of Visnapuu (an author who emigrated and was characterized in his later years by extreme reactionary inclinations) which ends with a plea to appreciate that which is good in Visnapuu's poetry without permitting the false steps of his personal life to overshadow it.[19] This may sound surprising, but it must be remembered that many changes have occurred in Estonia since the end of the Stalin era. Books by authors previously suppressed were published in the late 1950s. In the early 1960s boat transportation between Tallin and Finland was resumed with subsequent compilation and publication of Finnish-Estonian dictionaries and the resumption of literary contacts with Finland.[20]

Activities in this domain fall into the following classes:
1. Research in Estonian folklore,
2. Contacts with other Finno-Ugric peoples (especially the Finns and Hungarians), and
3. Awareness of Estonian literature through the end of the period of independence.

During 1972, many of the folklore-oriented activities were part of the jubilee preparations to promote a "united family" image through cultural exchange between Union republics, but activities with a uniquely Estonian inclination are also in evidence. There is work being done by the Ethnography Museum, both in publication and collection, with the announcement of a competition for materials concerning handicrafts, housing, agriculture, ship building and transportation, clothing, and folk customs and traditions in pre- and early Soviet times.21 The Academy of Sciences and the Society for the Mother Tongue are also involved in similar activities. The response to their vocabulary and place name collecting competition included over 9,000 word slips and 2,000 pages of dialect texts. Of particular interest is the entry from Tiit Siiv of Tallin about student speech and city slang which received a consolation prize, because it indicates not only interest in preserving language forms but also awareness of current developments in the speech of young Estonians.22 Another unusual aspect of current Estonian ethnography is the collection of materials in the Kreutzwald library gathered mostly in the 1950s by Jakob Nerman concerning the culture of the Estonians of the Caucasus and Crimea, descendants of serfs who moved to free government lands there in the middle of the nineteenth century.23

As may have been gathered from the discussion of language roles, the Finns figure most prominently among the related peoples from whom the Estonians can draw support for their reservoir of nationality material. It is difficult to estimate the present state of contacts between Estonia and the linguistically related Karelian ASSR. There has been some mention of articles on Estonia and by Estonians appearing in Karelian periodicals,24 but sources have generally been silent regarding Karelia.

In regard to Finland, during the period from November 1972 to March 1973, one novel, one childrens' book, and one book on mass communications were translated from Finnish and published in Soviet Estonia, and a number of contemporary Finnish poems were published in Looming in July 1972.25 It should not be assumed, however, that Estonians uncritically accept all aspects of the contacts touching on the Finnish connection. A sharp awareness of Estonian-Finnish cultural differences is shown by Oskar Kruus in his review of a theatrical production of Niskamäe Naised (The Women of Niskamaki) by Hella Vuolijoki, who was born in Estonia, studied in Finland, and wrote in the languages of both. In commenting on how Elo Kask plays the part of Loviisa as if she were an Estonian peasant rather than the wife of a well-to-do Finnish farmer, he is lead to wonder whether Estonians should not after all interpret Finnish drama into an Estonian framework as the Hungarians reinterpreted the Finnish national epic Kalevala into a Hungarian one.26

Drawing only on Estonian sources, it would seem that these exchanges with Finland are quite one-sided, with no mention of Estonian books translated into Finnish during the period in question and only about a half-dozen articles on Estonia appearing in Finnish magazines. This would ignore, however, the importance of Estonia to Finnic language scholarship in Finland, functioning as it does as the transmitting point for information on the Finno-Ugric, especially the Balto-Finnic, languages spoken in the USSR. A glance at the book reviews in Virittäjä, the Finnish quarterly of native language scholarship, reveals the lively interest with which Estonian linguistics is followed. The first issue of 1971, for example, contains reviews of four books on the Estonian language—three from Soviet Estonia and one emigre.

Although Hungarian and Estonian are not in the least mutually intelligible, connections with Hungary also serve the purpose of reinforcing Estonian nationality identity. The visit in September of the Budapest theater "Thalia," which presented its stage adaption of Kalevala to a warmly receptive Estonian audience, was discussed by E. Tinn, who said that the epic and its fantastic stories are not only a collection of well-preserved memorials of the past but "it is us all," stating that one can see the importance more clearly from a distance, and suggesting an epic exchange of sorts involving the presentation of Kalevipoeg (Son of Kalev, the Estonian national epic) on Russian and Latvian stages and of Russian bylini in Estonia.27 Another example is the celebration in Tartu on the 150th anniversary of the birth of Sándor Petőfi, the Hungarian poet. Hungarian apparently provides a diffuse sort of Finno-Ugric moral encouragement, but little in the way of concrete example.

The third aspect of Estonians' passive awareness of their cultural past is in about the same situation as the previous two. Again, the weak state of pressure appearing at the present time can be best understood in comparison to earlier stages:

> The Soviets not only impose Russian culture on the Balts but they make important decisions in the remaining small area of the national literature . . . deciding what is artistically acceptable and what is not acceptable. Thus in the two-volume anthology of Estonian poetry translated into Russian and published by the State Publishing House for Belles-Lettres in Leningrad and Moscow in 1959, the greatest poets of Estonia, Marie Under and Gustav Suits, are not included. In the . . . introduction to this anthology, Marie Under is not mentioned at all and Gustav Suits' name appears only once and that [sic] negatively.28

Considering the works of these two authors as indicative of the treatment of pre-Soviet Estonian literature as a whole, let us turn to their more recent situation. In 1957 and 1958, anthologies of Marie Under's poetry were published for the first time in Soviet Estonia[29] and in 1959 one of Suits' works followed.[30] At the present time, their works are not only available but referred to with praise, even by good Party members.[31] The rehabilitation of Visnapuu in 1966 has been referred to above; it is not clear whether his later works are available, although passages were reprinted in the article cited above. There is little mention of current emigre poetry or fiction, except for one article dealing with the decline of Estonian emigre literature which is attributed in part to its failure to adopt the principles of socialist realism.[32] On the other hand, attacks on pre-Soviet Estonian literature are also lacking and in some, admittedly minor, fields such as book graphics[33] and the study of the history of Estonian publishing[34] the achievements of the period of independence are referred to with pride. Linguistically and critically oriented emigre works, in any case, seem to be available: in an article on Estonian family names Saareste's Kaunis Emakeel (Beautiful Mother Tongue, 1952) and Suits' Eesti Kirjanduslugu (History of Estonian Literature, 1953), both published in Sweden, are given as sources.[35]

In short, Estonians show a lively interest in their folk culture, one aspect of which (dialectology) contributes to the standards of language planning and maintenance on the Republic level; they have some degree of contact with Finno-Ugric peoples outside the Soviet Union (Finns, Hungarians, and their emigres); and they have access to their own pre-Soviet literature. In looking for signs of integrative pressure in this field, one can only attempt to speculate about whether the extent of any of the aforementioned three fields of activity would be comparatively greater if Estonia were not part of the Soviet Union. Although it seems likely that they (at least the second two) would, there no longer seems to be a concerted attempt in Estonia to sever connections with the past completely. The diffuse nature of pressure at this level makes it difficult to isolate particular groups.

SOCIALIST REALISM AND ESTONIAN
LITERATURE

The next step is to determine whether the Estonians are actually utilizing their linguistic and historical resources to produce anything which could be characterized as a nationality-distinctive literature. This is a particularly significant question for two reasons. First, passive recognition of and access to nationality culture cannot be considered an effective expression of nationality consciousness until it is incorporated into the course of ongoing, productive literature. This is related to the second factor, that current literary production is the area in which a distinct, overt integrative pressure is being exerted. The pressure in this case is a continuous flow of directives originating from the central government and Communist party and transmitted through the Estonian party, Ministry of Culture, and artists' unions requiring conformity to the principles of socialist realism in literature and application of these principles in literary criticism.

This may require some explanation, because socialist realism is apparently not usually considered in conjunction with the nationality question. The following definition of socialist realism, given by the First Union-wide Congress of Soviet Writers in 1934, bears no overt mention of nationality:

> Socialist realism is the basic method of Soviet literature and literary criticism. It demands of the artist the truthful, historically concrete representation of reality in its revolutionary development. Moreover, the truthfulness and historical concreteness of the artistic representation of reality must be linked with the task of ideological transformation and education of workers in the spirit of socialism.[36]

In practice, however, it appears that there are three interpretations of the doctrine of socialist realism. The first may be characterized as the nationality blind interpretation. This is perhaps the most idealistic (one might even say impractical), ignoring the nationality question not as a conscious integrative maneuver but because it (or, more properly, its adherents) regard(s) the principles of socialist realism as applying to all socialist peoples in a multinational state. The second, which shall be termed the Russian model interpretation, hinges on the key term "historically concrete" in the above passage. According to this, the Russians, by virtue of being chronologically the first socialist people, have an inherent position of primary significance in socialist-realist literature. This view is reflected, for example, in a recent article reprinted from Literaturnaia gazeta in which, while dealing primarily with foreign responses and reactions to Soviet literature, the author states that Lenin in 1918 saw the RSFSR as a literary model for peoples of all lands.[37]

The third possible interpretation, indications of which are not to be found in the passage above but in more recent sources, is the antilocalist interpretation, which posits the incompatibility of socialist realism and localism (nationality cultural characteristics). An example of this in recent times were G. Markov's comments at the USSR Writers' Union meeting on literary criticism against un-Marxist treatment of old culture and attempts to conserve nationality

21

characteristics, made in connection with statements on the problems of journalism in a multinational state.38 In other words, socialist realism can be considered overtly opposed to nationality consciousness when aspects of nationality culture and history are not made to conform to a Marxist interpretation.

We may therefore establish a set of interrelationships between the three interpretations of socialist realism and the nationality question (Figure 5).

Given that this kind of pressure exists (and that it does can be seen from the many issues of Sirp ja Vasar that begin with translations of articles from Voprosy literatury, Literaturnaia gazeta, and Pravda, and statements by government and Party entities on the Republic and the Union-wide levels dealing with just this): what is its effect? First, is there universal voluntary obedience to it? In other words, have Estonian writers abandoned attempts, or lost the desire, to produce an above-ground nationality literature? Second, are there any attempts to enforce the directives, such as a refusal to publish works which do not conform to them, which are effective?

A specific example of how groups of different levels are involved in pressure for integration through applying socialist realism to literature can be seen in the account of a meeting of the Estonian Writers' Union held to evaluate the tasks set forth in a recent directive from the Central Committee of the Communist party of Estonia concerning compliance with Union-wide programs and to discuss work in fulfilling the directive of the Central Committee of the Communist party of the USSR on literature and criticism.39

The same account, however, also shows by implication how Estonian literature has apparently not been fulfilling Party wishes in recent times. At the meeting, Vladimir Beekman said that Soviet Estonian literature does not give meaning to or reveal in sufficient depth society's dynamic and varied life, the Soviet peoples' devotion to Communism, and the Party's leading role and great constructive

FIGURE 5

Socialist Realism and Nationality

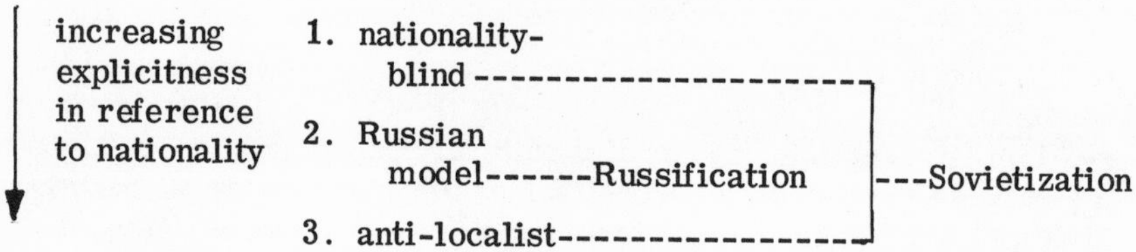

deeds, and that criticism lacks sociopolitical analyses of literary
works and exhibitions. He continues to say that there are too few
political and patriotic works in today's poetry and that the magazine
Looming (Art)*, while containing some good articles and translations
of important stories, still lacks portrayals of Soviet life and resistance
against the influences of Western fashion. Eduard Päll speaks in the
same vein, saying that although there is socialist-realist literature,
there are also works in which a picture of life is lacking. Furthermore, Päll notes that there are some extreme modernist experimen-
talists who say that socialist realism is obsolete and demand a literature apart from life, and whose inclinations are exemplified by an
internal orientation in literary criticism. Part of this self-criticism
may be due to a certain amount of overreaction by the members of
the Writer's Union in the face of a Party directive, rather than to
the condition of Estonian literature itself. It is too soon to see the
results of the whole affair, but to judge from the case of the Cinema-
tographers' Union last fall, the actual steps taken can be as small
as the reaction is great.[40]

A more neutral appraisal of the state of Estonian literature
appeared in a report on a meeting called by Sirp ja Vasar to discuss
tendencies in current prose. The consensus was that Estonian fiction
of the 1970s is much more diversified than that of the previous decade,
with the old publitsistlik (sociopolitical journalistic) novel being replaced, in part, by nontraditional psychological and philosophical
novels. At the meeting it was declared that "literature has given
up its independence and gone from the illustration of golden-age
dogmatic ideas to the other extreme . . . of portraying antidogmatic
ideas and becoming the mouthpiece of its own style of ideas," adding
that this is not a peculiarity of Estonian literature but a property of
contemporary world literature in general.[41]

There is, of course, much in Estonian literature that does conform to the dictates of socialist realism. One such book which appeared
recently is Egon Rannet's Kivid ja leib (Stones and Bread), the first
part of a proposed trilogy dealing with the social events of the years
from 1931 to 1955. This work fills the need, in the opinion of one
reviewer,[42] for a book about life in an Estonian village of the socialist
period, complete with a factory director who, although a good admin-
istrator, runs into problems in his work because he has insufficient
theoretical knowledge.

Of the writers who do not fulfill the requirements of socialist
realism, two are useful to discuss because they both published books

---

*A publication of the Writers' Union of which Beekman himself
is an editor.

recently which could be considered reflective of certain aspects of a nationality literature, and because they figured sufficiently in the local press in other ways to give some kind of personal profile. One, Jaan Kaplinski, is a poet who seems to regard his task with great dedication. The other, Teet Kallas, is a prose writer whose salient feature seems to be, at least on the surface, a devout dedication to frivolity.

The appearance of Kallas' novel Heliseb-Kõliseb (Jingle-Jangle) was heralded by an interview with the author, in which he stated that his new book is essentially a fairytale for grownups and that its intent is not to raise or handle deep social problems but to show that reality and fantasy are not separable from each other.[43] The review also emphasizes the juxtaposition of reality and fantasy, implying that Heliseb-Kõliseb is to the twentieth century what Kalevala was to its era in its treatment of the relationship of magic to life. In closing, he remarks that "if Fa-Fa (Fantoom and Fatme)* do not organize a conspiracy against the author, there is no reason why Teet Kallas should not quickly satisfy our reading public's desires."[44] In short, Kallas seems to be able to ignore the fact that socialist realism directives are raining down around him while embedding many concretely Estonian details in a matrix of fantasy.

Jaan Kaplinski is involved in both writing and literary criticism. His article about children's poetry criticized the use of such Russian and German metrical devices as abab or abcb rhyme schemes and the seven or eight syllable line in children's verse, urging the adoption of forms more natural to Estonian with its complicated word structure and shortage of unforced rhymes. He went on to attack the choice of subject matter, with its gilded oversentimentalizing of childhood, mentioning by name L. Tungel's Rahvaste sõpruse karneval (Carnival of Peoples' Friendship) as an example of this. One of his most surprising proposals is the suggestion that South-Estonian dialect poetry be written for children from that region in order to teach them language skills, an important function of children's poetry which can only be accomplished in one's mother language.[45] This article was awarded recognition as one of the best to appear in Sirp ja Vasar in 1972.

The review of Kaplinski's book Valge joon võrumaa kohale (White line over Võrumaa), a collection of his poetry from the years 1967-1968, is not only favorable but quite revealing as well. The reviewer says that while Kaplinski's own personality and logical system appear in his poetry, he is "not one of those men who explicitly and didactically try to instill their own thoughts." The poet's "route to

---

*Two of the novel's characters

resolution," he continues, consists of three stages: from person to person, from person back to nature, and by way of nature to understand and make a future for humanity. Sometimes, he says, this scheme is interpreted as doubt toward the authority of social regulations, but such criticism is "narrowminded and antisocial" because Kaplinski does not claim to delineate a path for everyone by his poetic-philosophical speculation.[46] It can be seen that Kaplinsky, more seriously than Kallas, embodies much the same elements: nonconformity with the dictates of socialist realism and a deep specific interest in Estonia.

Two conclusions can be drawn. First, Kaplinski and Kallas are not alone. The reviewers seem virtually unanimously sympathetic, and there are indications that other writers are following a similar path, although they did not come into the spotlight with such prominence during the period studied. Second, the groups responsible for the promulgation of socialist realism decrees do not seem to be taking steps to see that these decrees are adhered to. Such indifference to the rules reaches even to the extent of failure on the part of government publishing houses to reject nonconforming materials.

A summary of the interaction in verbal-arts-related activities in Estonia is given diagrammatically in Figure 6.

Why does there seem to be such a relatively great permissiveness in Estonia toward the development of a nationality literature and its prerequisites, language maintenance and awareness of cultural roots? An explanation may lie partly in the size of Estonia.

> The Estonians were a small people, dependent on both the Czarist government . . . and on the Baltic-German aristocracy [in the nineteenth century]. Their status was by no means a favourable one from the point of view of the development of the natural culture; and to a certain extent their attempts at self-expression were made possible only by the conflict of interests between the Baltic Germans and the central authority of the state. Their position was a precarious one, and the whole of the Estonian national movement was little more than a slight local disturbance within the huge framework of the Czarist Russian Empire.[47]

It is an even smaller ripple today in the even larger Soviet Union. With formal economic, political, and military integration virtually complete, and a steadily increasing Russian population in Estonia creating the need for increasing use of the Russian language in professional fields, it would hardly be worth the trouble to make sure that every trace of what could become a nationality literature is eradicated.

25

FIGURE 6

Language and Literature in Estonia

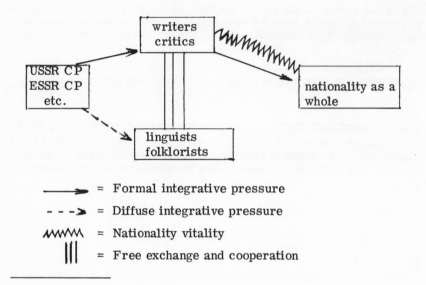

⟶	= Formal integrative pressure
- - -➤	= Diffuse integrative pressure
∧∧∧∧∧	= Nationality vitality
|||	= Free exchange and cooperation

Viewed as a part of the Soviet West, the case of Estonia indicates that a multitude of variables contributes to the creation of a state of affairs in which the verbal arts can function as an effective focal point for divisiveness. Although clearly sufficient, the following circumstances are perhaps not all necessary prerequisites. They may, however, indicate some of the reserves that are necessary to be drawn on.

First is the presence of an intellectual tradition. Although the age and the Western orientation of Estonian scholarship has been at times overestimated, there has been an indigenous literature with a nationality orientation that developed during the nineteenth century and peaked during the period of independence. Coincident with this is a tradition of language maintenance with an expressed intention of keeping the language pure of foreign lexical items and grammatical patterns (of which the latter is perhaps more important to Estonian than it would be to an Indo-European language in a similar situation). A third is a non-Russian or non-Soviet focus for and contributor to nationality awareness. In this case, Estonia has not only Finland, Hungary, and emigre centers abroad, but also a historical and cultural affinity with Germany not unlike that of Lithuania with Poland.

In addition, there must be an element of popular resonance, conscious and unconscious. The latter can be inferred from the high degree of nationality language retention in Estonia and the apparent lack of stigma connected with the nationality identity. A nationality literature could possibly exist with no popular response, but it could not be said to be an effective force if its audience were virtually identical with its authorship. The last variable to be isolated is institutional tolerance, which can be discerned in Estonia in practice, if not in principle.

The Soviet West shows considerable diversity in the cultural sphere with respect to all these variables. Although some of its republics are, for example, contiguous to East European countries, not all have contacts with them which could be considered as a factor leading to divisiveness with respect to the center.

Although it is clear that not all of these factors need to be present to render possible the use of the verbal arts as a force for nationality consciousness (intuitively, an external focus would seem to be less essential than popular resonance, for example), one might expect the viability and efficacy of such a force to be more or less proportional to the degree to which at least some of these five variables are fulfilled. Estonia typifies a situation in which these factors are all fulfilled, thus providing the foundations for an antihomogeneous literature indicative of nationality vitality. Application of these criteria to other nationalities of the Soviet West may establish an approximate gauge of their potential to produce a centrifugal literature.

NOTES

1. A. Rannit, "A note on Estonian humor: can literature be national?", Journal of Baltic Studies, 3, No. 3/4 (1972), p. 171f.

2. See E. Nirk, Estonian Literature (Tallin: Eesti Raamat, 1970), sections 2 and 3.

3. A. Raun and A. Saareste, Introduction to Estonian Linguistics (Wiesbaden: Otto Harrassowitz, 1965), p. 79f.

4. "Vene keel minu elus," Rahva Hääl, 28 Sept. 1972, p. 2.

5. Ibid.

6. T. Velliste, "Alguses oli tegu," Sirp ja Vasar, November 17, 1972, p. 5.

7. "NSVL 50: Rahvaste sõprus," Sirp ja Vasar, December 22, 1972, p. 2.

8. L. Püss, V. Miller, "Eesti kirjandus laias maailmas," Sirp ja Vasar, December 29, 1972, p. 11.

9. H. Meriste, "Vene sõnalaenudest eesti keeles," Sirp ja Vasar, December 22, 1972, p. 12.

10. "Keeleveerud," Sirp ja Vasar, November 24, 1972, p. 12.

11. H. Meriste, "Tükk tegu tõlkimisega," Sirp ja Vasar, January 26, 1973, p. 12.

12. H. Ernesaks, "Paar küsimust 'Valguse' peatoimetajale Helmuth Kasesalule," Sirp ja Vasar, February 2, 1973, p. 4.

13. Püss and Miller.

14. "Uusi raamatuid," Sirp ja Vasar, November 24, 1972, p. 15.

15. "Estica," Sirp ja Vasar, December 15, 1972, p. 14.

16. T. Vettik, "Suur Laul," Sirp ja Vasar, November 10, 1972, p. 10.

17. "Keeleveerud," Sirp ja Vasar, November 24, 1972, p. 12.

18. Ain Kaalep, "Terä sahind salven," Sirp ja Vasar, January 5, 1973, p. 5.

19. P. Rummo, "Henrik Visnapuu 3 isamaalaulu jälgedel," Keel ja Kirjandus, No. 7 (1966), p. 415.

20. For an account of post-Soviet interaction see G. Kurman, Literatures in Contact: Finland and Estonia (New York: Estonian Learned Society in America, 1972), Chapter 7.

21. "Etnograafilise materjali kogumise võistlus," Sirp ja Vasar, November 10, 1972, p. 14.

22. "Sõnavara ja kohanimide kogumise voistluselt," (ETA) Sirp ja Vasar, January 5, 1973, p. 15.

23. H. Tamme, "Kilde kultuuriloost: ühest kaukaasia eesti külade tundjast," Sirp ja Vasar, January 12, 1973, p. 12.

24. "Estica," Sirp ja Vasar, November 24, 1972, p. 4.

25. "Uusi Raamatuid," Sirp ja Vasar, November 3, 1972, p. 15.

26. O. Kruus" 'Niskamäe naised' P. Pinna nim. Rahvateatris," Sirp ja Vasar, February 23, 1973, p. 6.

27. E. Tinna, "My luchshe poniali sebia," Sovetskaia Estonia, September 24, 1972, p. 2.

28. A. Rannit, "The current state of Baltic literatures under Soviet Occupation," Testimony given before the Committee on Foreign Affairs Subcommittee on Europe of the United States Congress, Washington, D.C., January 27, 1964, p. 4.

29. Nirk, p. 399.

30. Nirk, p. 402.

31. "Õnnesoov Helene Johanile," Sirp ja Vasar, February 23, 1973, p. 5.

32. A. Saar, "Sotsialistlik realism—arengujooni ja probleeme," Sirp ja Vasar, November 3, 1972, p. 4.

33. R. Loodus, "1972. aasta raamatugraafikas," Sirp ja Vasar, January 19, 1973, p. 8.

34. "Estica," Sirp ja Vasar, November 24, 1972, p. 5.

35. Edgar Rajand and Helmut Tarand, "Meie perekonnanimide liigitamisest ja seletamisest," Keel ja Kirjandus, No. 7 (1966), p. 393f.

36. A. Tertz, "The Trial Begins" and "On Socialist Realism," (New York: Vintage, 1960), p. 148

37. J. Trushtshenko, "Sotsialistlik realism ja progressiivne kirjandus," Sirp ja Vasar, February 23, 1973, p. 2.

38. E. Lobu, "Kriitika osast kirjandusprotsessi arengus," Sirp ja Vasar, February 9, 1973, p. 2.

39. H. Kermik, "Rohkem konstruktiivset vaimu ja nõudlikkust!," Sirp ja Vasar, March 2, 1973, p. 2.

40. "Eesti kinematografistide liidu juhatuse pleenumilt," Sirp ja Vasar, November 10, 1972, p. 6f.

41. "Proosakirjanduse arengutendentse," Sirp ja Vasar, February 16, 1973, p. 2ff.

42. V. Leede, "Lugeja pilguga," Sirp ja Vasar, February 23, 1973, p. 4.

43. E. Maremäe, "Ilmus uus teos . . . ," Sirp ja Vasar, December 22, 1972, p. 5.

44. H. Puhvel, "Retsensioon-vevüü ehk ootamatu kohtumine voluriga," Sirp ja Vasar, February 2, 1973, p. 4.

45. J. Kaplinski, "Täiskasvanutele lastest," Sirp ja Vasar, November 17, 1972, p. 4.

46. H.-K. Hellat, "Etüüd rikkast tundeihnurist," Sirp ja Vasar, January 19, 1973, p. 4.

47. Nirk, p. 102.

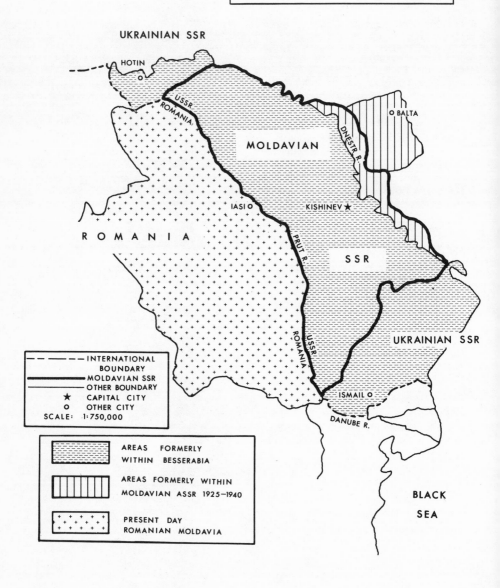

THE MOLDAVIA–BESSARABIA AREA

UKRAINIAN SSR

HOTIN

USSR
ROMANIA

MOLDAVIAN

O BALTA

DNESTR R.

IASI O

KISHINEV ★

ROMANIA

PRUT R.

SSR

ROMANIA
USSR

UKRAINIAN SSR

ISMAIL O

DANUBE R.

BLACK
SEA

- – – – – – INTERNATIONAL
               BOUNDARY
————— MOLDAVIAN SSR
————— OTHER BOUNDARY
   ★   CAPITAL CITY
   O   OTHER CITY
SCALE: 1:750,000

AREAS FORMERLY
WITHIN BESSERABIA

AREAS FORMERLY WITHIN
MOLDAVIAN ASSR 1925–1940

PRESENT DAY
ROMANIAN MOLDAVIA

3

MOLDAVIANS OR
ROMANIANS?
Nicholas Dima

Within the last three decades, since the Soviet Union finally
incorporated Moldavia into its territory, an effort has been made by
the Soviet government to separate Moldavians from any Romanian
influence. At the same time, other pressures have been exerted upon
the Moldavians in an attempt to create a new nationality identity,
distinct from the former Romanian identity. In this study, we will
examine evidence drawn from the press of the Moldavian Soviet
Socialist Republic (MSSR) to ascertain the extent to which these pressures for a distinct, Moldavian, identity are currently being emphasized, as well as the degree to which Moldavians are accepting the
concept of ethnic distinctiveness. In order to achieve this objective,
this investigation will focus upon one sector within Moldavian society,
the humanist intellectuals.

This study entails linguistic analysis and some social, historical,
cultural, and demographic interpretations. The study also attempts
to trace the interaction between the group of political leaders of
Soviet Moldavia, advocating homogenization of Moldavians into Soviet
society, and the Moldavian intellectuals, struggling to maintain their
nationality culture.

Evidence is gathered from the Soviet Moldavian periodicals
Moldova Socialistă from November 1972 to March 1973, and selec-
tively, from Comunistul Moldovei, Nistru, and Tinerimea Moldovei.
Data have also been utilized from back issues of Cultura and Moldova
Socialistă, as well as from other available publications.

THE BACKGROUND OF MOLDAVIA:
A CONTESTED LAND

The Soviet Socialist Republic of Moldavia, or Bessarabia, as
it was formerly known, is a historically much disputed territory

located in the southwest corner of the Soviet West, between Romania and the Ukraine. The country consists mainly of plains with some low hills in the center, and it is an excellent agricultural area. Although the area of Moldavia represents only .22 percent of the total land surface of the Soviet Union, and its population of 3.5 million inhabitants is only 1.4 percent of the total Soviet population, Moldavian agriculture accounts for very significant shares of the total Soviet farm production, particularly in such commodities as wine, tobacco, canned goods, grain, vegetable oils, and many other items.[1] In general, industry is poorly developed in the MSSR, although recently the Republic has undergone some industrialization.

Historically, present day Soviet Moldavia is the eastern part of the former Moldavia, one of the two Romanian Principalities that were formed during the thirteenth and fourteenth centuries. During the fifteenth and sixteenth centuries, the Principality of Moldavia went through a period of general prosperity. Its enemies at that time were the Ottoman Empire to the south and the Tatars from beyond the Dnestr to the east. The Russian Empire was still distant and not yet a threat to Moldavian territory. In the year 1511, and again in 1634, no longer able to resist Ottoman pressure, Moldavia was forced to sign a treaty with the Porte. Although the treaty was one of vassalage, its terms were honorable; among other things, Turkey bound itself to preserve Moldavian independence and territory.[2] However, in 1812, following a Russo-Turkish war, Turkey acted against the treaty, relinquishing to Russia the eastern half of Moldavia, known as Bessarabia, although this area had never been part of the Turkish Empire. According to Russian estimates, the population of that territory was 482,000 inhabitants in 1817, and 86.7 percent of these were enumerated by the Russian Government as Moldavians or Romanians.[3] Regarding the annexation of Bessarabia, Karl Marx specifically denied the legality of the Turkish cession of Bessarabia to Russia, noting that the ceded territory was not actually within the Ottoman Empire.[4]

The territory under discussion remained a bone of contention in this part of Europe, and changed hands between Romania and Russia several times before being permanently incorporated into the Czarist Empire. Concerning this reannexation, Engels wrote in 1890:

> Finland is Finnish, Poland is Polish, Bessarabia is Romanian. There is no question of bringing together various populations dispersed and related, who could be called Russian. This is a brutal and undisguised conquest of foreign territories, purely and simply a theft.[5]

Soviet historians writing on this subject generally agree that Bessarabia and Western Georgia were given to Russia under the treaty of Bucharest, concluded in 1812, and that the "union" of Bessarabia with Russia was a historically "progressive" act, for it provided better opportunities for the economic development of the Bessarabian population.[6]

Just how advantageous the incorporation into Russia was for the local population can be seen from its consequences. A contemporary Soviet historian has written that the Czarist regime attempted forced Russification; among other things, teaching in the Moldavian language was forbidden.[7] Actually, in 1871, the Moldavian language was completely eliminated from all schools.[8] As a direct consequence, at the time of the first modern Russian census, in 1897, the Moldavians were found to be the least literate people in their own nationality territory.[9] Since that time, Moldavians have remained the least educated group both in Romania between the two World Wars, and in the Soviet West after World War II.

Deeply dissatisfied, Moldavians and the other nationalities of Bessarabia revolted in 1917, formed the Council of State (Sfatul Tării) and declared the region autonomous. On January 24, 1918, on the anniversary of the day on which the two Romanian Principalities had united in 1859 to form modern Romania, the Council of State declared Bessarabia an independent republic, and in March 1918, it voted union with Romania.

After the Paris Conference in 1920, the Romanian parliament ratified the union, but it proved to be a short one. In 1940, following the Hitler-Stalin pact and then again at the end of World War II, Bessarabia was occupied by the Soviets for the last time. Based mostly on the territory and population of the former Romanian province of Bessarabia, the Soviet authorities created what is today the MSSR (see Map 2). Until about 1955, Moldavia was an agricultural hinterland, the indigenous Moldavians being almost exclusively peasants. However, in the last two decades, a young generation of Moldavian intellectuals has matured, bringing with them new ideas and a vital sense of nationality. These young intellectuals have "rediscovered" their identity and have become eager to strengthen their own nationality, despite the pressure for integration and homogenization within the Soviet West which is exercised through the local Party and government.

SOVIET POLICY REGARDING THE MOLDAVIANS

As a step toward a closer merger with other Soviet nationalities, and perhaps as part of integration of Moldavia within the Soviet West, constant pressure is being directed upon the Moldavians to encourage the creation of a new, separate nationality in order to draw them away from Romanian-based identity and irredentism. However, as we shall discuss later, the entire cultural life of Moldavia is so closely connected with its larger Romanian past that the two cannot be separated. Evidence substantiating this contention is found in all contemporary Soviet Moldavian publications.

Writing about their own past is one of the most troublesome problems for Soviet Moldavian writers. Generally, the historical pattern described by these writers is identical, regardless of the nature of the medium or the audience to which the message is directed. Authors usually begin with the Russian "liberation" of Moldavia from Turkish rule. Then, the union with Romania is characterized as "aggression" and "exploitation," and finally, the "happiness" of membership in the Soviet Union is emphasized.[10] In general, Romania is rarely mentioned, and if so, then only briefly, as having transformed the former Bessarabia into a colony.[11]

However, the problem is not solved by hiding the past, and more definitive positions were taken by the Soviet authorities. One of the most explicit attitudes was expressed by the First Secretary of the Moldavian Communist party. In 1966 he wrote a long article acknowledging that many Moldavians demonstrate an immature, uncomprehending, nationalistic, and retrograde attitude, that they are still the victims of foreign "misinformation," and have not completely broken with the "capitalistic past."[12] In other words, the young students do not seem to have forgotten the past in spite of the "benefits" of the new status of Moldavia. As recently as late 1971, the words "Long Live Romania. We want to be with Romania" were found written on the walls of the Press House in Kishinev, the capital of the MSSR.[13]

In an effort to convince Moldavians that they are a separate nationality, Soviet Moldavian writers produce various articles on the topic. An historian, for instance, in a long article directed against all those who deny that Moldavian is a separate nationality, unexpectedly recognizes a common origin, history, and culture with Romania, but attempts to enlarge this similarity with many other Southeastern European peoples. Furthermore, the author avoids the word "Romanian," replacing it in the historical context, with the word "Wallachian," and insists upon the distinctiveness of the Moldavian people, rather than upon the common nationality identity of all Romanians. Actually, the author has essentially recapitulated Romanian history. Nevertheless, basing his argument upon some vague speculations, he concludes that Moldavians have a history and some traits of their own and, therefore, whoever denies the distinctiveness of the Moldavian nationality is a "capitalist instigator."[14]

Little can be done about the past, but a great deal more can be attempted about the present. In its current form, Soviet Moldavia is completely isolated from Romania, socially and politically. Even the very words "Romania" or "Romanian" are unmentionable, and Soviet Moldavian writers have developed a special skill to write about their Romanian past and avoid such sensitive terms. To make certain that such errors are not committed, Moldova Socialistă, the Party's daily paper, carries very little news about Romania. When the Vietnam cease-fire agreement was reached in 1973, for example, Moldova Socialistă printed the official reactions of all the socialist and even some Western countries, but not a single reference to the Romanian position was in evidence.[15]

The cultural heritage of the past is an even more delicate subject. Soviet Moldavia has produced very little in the sphere of intellectual life, and its folk art is inseparable from the Romanian variety. Attempting to prove that Soviet Moldavia has a cultural character of its own, a writer cites as Moldavian such popular ballads as "Gruia," "Novac," "Iancu Jianu," and the like, all of them generally recognized as Romanian. The same author arrives at the conclusion that Moldavians have a popular culture of their own and are therefore a nationality.[16] Certainly, some of this folk art is Moldavian, but it is virtually impossible, because of the common historical past of Moldavians and Romanians, to distinguish between the two. In their attempt to foster a Moldavian identity, the Soviet authorities have sought to weaken the Romanian composition of the Republic. On the one hand many Moldavians have been deported or encouraged to leave their Republic; on the other hand these Moldavians have been replaced by hundreds of thousands of Russians and Ukrainians.

Recent issues of Cultura contain many letters to the editor from Moldavians now residing in Central Asia or Siberia, usually in reference to the location of relatives displaced by World War II or other events.[17] Very often, young school or university graduates are invited to work or to settle permanently in various places of employment, often at considerable distances from Moldavia. In 1969, for example, 3,000 young skilled and unskilled Moldavian workers went to Tiumen, in West Siberia, to assist in the construction of a railroad.[18] At present, there is considerable evidence of "voluntary" departure to Kazakhstan, which is referred to as a "sister republic." An announcement printed regularly in Moldova Socialistă, reads as follows:

> The State Council of Labor Force of the Moldavian SSR invites peasant families, workers, and clerks, to move and settle permanently in Kazakhstan. They will be provided with free transportation for their families and belongings and with a financial incentive. They will also

35

be provided with jobs, houses free of rent for two years,
fuel for their houses for two years, and cash to buy a
cow, plus other benefits. Unskilled workers are also
invited to work on different construction sites which
also have many advantages. . .[19]

At the same time Russians and others are entering the MSSR
and taking advantage of the best job opportunities. Although Russians
and Ukrainians make up 23 percent of the population of Soviet Moldavia,
they hold 65 percent of the jobs in industry and services, while Moldavians and the other local nationalities make up 77 percent of the
population and hold only 33 percent of all such jobs. It appears that
some Moldavians have demonstrated their discontent concerning this
situation, and the Party's First Secretary intervened. He stated that
the working class of the Republic increased from 8,000 to 430,000
during the Soviet period, and that there are at present 627,000 blue
and white collar workers in Moldavia, including 264,000 Moldavians.
The First Secretary calls this a "Leninist solution of the problem of
nationalities," and even states that "it would be a mistake to give
priority to national cadres, no matter what their professional qualifications may be."[20]

A Soviet demographer recognized that Russians and Ukrainians,
who constituted only 16 percent of the Republic's population in 1944,
have increased greatly since then because of the large influx of
migrants, mostly into the cities.[21] His data and data from the 1959
and 1970 Soviet censuses make it possible to calculate the expected
population by ethnic group and estimate in-migration from the residual.
The result is that, as of the 1970 census, there were in the MSSR
close to 500,000 more Russians and Ukrainians than could have been
accounted for by natural increase, a figure approximating the net
migration of these ethnic groups into the Republic between 1945 and
1970.

We have also calculated the total population of Moldavia by ethnic
group to estimate in-migration between the Soviet census years of
1959 and 1970. Again, during this period there was an excess of
130,000 Russians and Ukrainians above that expected from natural
increase alone. Actually, the difference is probably much greater,
because the projection was made on the basis of the rate of natural
increase of all Russians and Ukrainians in the Soviet Union. However,
since the Russians and Ukrainians in the MSSR are mostly urban,
their rate of natural increase is no doubt lower than the corresponding
rates for the USSR as a whole, which also includes the rural population.

Because most of the Russians and Ukrainians settled in urban
areas, the population of Moldavian cities increased by 5.2 percent

per year between the two censuses, compared to the Soviet average of 2.9 percent per year. However, as an American economist has noted: "relations between nations are often profoundly affected by long-run forces, over which men can exercise only limited control in the short run."[22] One of these "long-run forces" was the high fertility and natural increase of the Moldavians, because of which the inflow of Russians and Ukrainians into the Republic failed to diminish the Moldavian component in the population. Accounting for 65 percent of the population of the MSSR in 1970, there is a sufficient population base of Moldavians for the maintenance of national expression and a Moldavian nationality culture in their Republic. (See Data Appendix I.)

Nevertheless, as a consequence of the inflow of Russians and due to the desire of the Soviet government for effective control, there is a disproportionate Russian presence at all levels of social, political economic, and cultural activity. In the political realm, Party membership was only 19 per thousand among Moldavians in 1960 and 64 per thousand among Russians on a Union-wide basis.[23] Actually, in Moldavia the disproportion is probably much higher in the favor of Russians. Consequently, Russian political representation is dominant in all top positions. In a recent political commentary, 17 Party and government leaders of Moldavia are listed, and only 5 of them have Moldavian names.[24] Furthermore, many of these non-Moldavian political leaders seem to view positions in the MSSR only as a step toward higher positions in the Soviet hierarchy. Leonid Brezhnev, who was the First Secretary of the Moldavian Communist Party under Stalin (1950-52), illustrates this process.[25]

Economically, the MSSR is only an administrative unit and has no national character. All indications point toward the integration of the Republic into the Soviet economy. Ideologically, the population is subject to strong indoctrination, with standard topics printed in neverending articles. All messages seem to be directed toward more uniformity and greater integration into the Soviet Union, toward bringing all nationalities together, and toward making them more "Soviet." In the case of the Moldavians, the stress is always placed upon their "common" destiny with that of the other Soviet peoples, in an attempt to erase completely the Romanian past. At the same time, the Party controls all aspects of this integrative pressure, from agriculture to the Writer's Union, asserting itself directly whenever necessary. Thus, the Party's representative intervened at a meeting of Moldavian writers, urging them to find inspiration for their work in socialist realism, in other words, work and the production of young Communists.[26] Recently, the fourth Union-wide Conference of the Soviet Teachers of Russian was held in Kishinev. The Moldavian Party representative greeted the delegates and urged them to improve their work, and to teach Russian better and faster to the non-Russian nationalities.[27]

The Moldavian case is an ambiguous one within the Soviet West. Some nationalities of the Soviet West, such as the Ukrainians, Belorussians, and others have their own republics where most of their people reside and where they have their cultural centers. Others, nationalities such as the Poles and Jews, have their cultural centers outside the Soviet Union, with no Soviet republic of their own. Unlike all the others, the Moldavians have their own Soviet republic, but their cultural core is outside the USSR, in neighboring Romania. This situation naturally results in irredentist tensions. Therefore, to a certain degree, Moldavians are allowed to express their nationality character as "Moldavian" but never as Romanian. Yet to what degree Moldavian?

THE QUESTION OF THE "MOLDAVIAN" LANGUAGE

An interesting aspect of the topic is the evolution of the Moldavian language during the last 25 years. Practically speaking, the present literary language is identical with Romanian, except that the alphabet is Cyrillic. However, the manner in which intellectuals employ the language in their writings reflects a tension that has existed for a number of years. Under Stalin, the authorities tried to impose an artificial language, with many Russian loanwords, local expressions, and archaic Romanian words of Slavonic origin. Moldavians who dared to express themselves in the Romanian literary language would be publicly reprimanded, as they were in 1949 in the journal Voprosy filosofii: "The Moldavian nationalists tried to drag artistocratic drawing-room words into their language."[28] Since then, the language has changed a great deal. In a recent article dealing with the translation of Marx, the author places side by side the German original, a French translation, the Romanian (Bucharest) translation and four Moldavian translations from 1948, 1953, 1962 and 1972.[29] It is instructive to note gradual changes in "Moldavian" language toward a "perfect" Romanian in the span of only a quarter of a century (see Appendix to this Chapter).

In a review of hundreds of articles on different fields, only a few Slavonic words (such as: truda, norod and slujba), now on the point of disappearing from literary Romanian, a few local expressions, and five Russian loanwords foreign to literary Romanian were in evidence. At the same time, many neologisms were apparent, none of them Russian. The majority of neologisms are taken from Romanian, such as: cineast, peliculă, autoservire, secventă, and frigider. A

38

few, such as poetesǎ, seem to be taken from French, and some others are locally formed from Romance roots, such as salutabil, material filmic and crengian (from the name of the poet I. Creangǎ). The most important point in this regard is that these innovations have been introduced from within by the young generation of Moldavian intellectuals.

THE SOVIET CREATION OF A MOLDAVIAN LITERATURE

Literature is naturally based upon a language, and since the classical literature to which Soviet Moldavian authors refer as "Moldavian" is entirely Romanian, the case for Moldavian distinctiveness in this area is even more artificial. There are countless articles about the elite of Romanian literature, Eminescu, Creangǎ, Alexandri, Ureche, Costin, Neculce, and others, without whom Romanian literature would not exist. These authors are from that part of Moldavia which today is within Romania, and many of them never even set foot in what is today Soviet Moldavia. Nevertheless, they are considered Moldavians by Soviet writers. Consequently, whenever present-day Soviet Moldavians write anything about these authors, they find it impossible to separate Moldavian culture from Romanian.

For example, in an article about Ion Creangǎ, the greatest Romanian writer for children (whom the Soviet Moldavians also claim as the greatest Moldavian writer for children), the author discusses his Memories from Childhood without even mentioning where Creangǎ was born and where he spent his childhood. Actually, Creangǎ was born in Romanian Moldavia and spent all his life in Romania. Furthermore, writing about Creangǎ's short story The Old Man John and the Union, the author omits the second part of the title because it refers to the Union of Moldavia with Wallachia which preceded the formation of modern Romania. Nevertheless, the author ends his article by praising the great writer, and expresses his deepest respect in a language indistinguishable from that of the Romanian Academy.[30]

There is evidently considerable pressure upon Moldavian writers to assert that they are Moldavians and nothing else. Why Moldavian? One can only speculate. Perhaps the Soviet leadership views the present Moldavian status as only a temporary measure designed to break away from the Romanian past. Moldavians themselves may find it more convenient, at least for the present, to assert their nationality with the hope of eventually claiming Romanian nationality. Indeed, there is more and more evidence that the Moldavian language is actually Romanian, though this fact is never directly stated in the Soviet press. There is more research, more desire to rediscover the past and to affirm it on the part of Soviet Moldavian intellectuals. Artists recently produced a movie about Dimitrie Cantemir, a former prince of Moldavia prior to the Russian annexation who sided with Russia in the Russo-Turkish war of 1711, and, when Russia lost the war, fled to St. Petersburg. The article about the movie emphasized that Cantemir was one of the great European intellectuals of his time, and only his death prevented him from becoming the president of the St. Petersburg Academy. The article mentions many of Cantemir's writings, and even refers to his history of the Romano-Moldo-Vlachs, whom he considered a single people. Although incapable of delimiting the concept of Moldavian, the author of the article declares Cantemir to be a Moldavian.[31]

There is presently fervent activity in the collection and publication of folk music. A Soviet publishing house recently issued an album of 500 folk songs, of which 449 are Moldavian, the others being songs of other ethnic groups of the MSSR. The author of a review article concerning this collection notes that such a work has not been published since the nineteenth century, when the first collection of Moldavian songs was published in Iaşi. Again, the author does not mention that Iaşi is the historical capital of the Romanian province of Moldavia. Further, the author lists scores of names of folk songs such as "doina," "miorița," "sîrba," "bătuta" and many others, all of them Romanian. Most of these are so generally Romanian in character that not one of the Romanian provinces could claim them as their own. Yet, they are presented here as Moldavian.[32]

At the same time, there are hundreds of institutions, schools, and ensembles in the Moldavian SSR which have pure Romanian names. Hardly any of them have a special connection with Soviet Moldavia. For example, the Pedogogical Institute in Kishinev is called "Ion Creangă"; the corresponding institution in Beltsi is "Alexandru Russo," and the Kishinev School of Art is named "G. Muzicescu"; all three named after leading Romanian intellectuals. The popular folk ensembles also all have Romanian names such as "Vîntulețul," "Flueraşul," "Lăutarul," "Mărţişorul" and the like. Consequently, the Romanian presence is steadily growing in the Moldavian SSR.

There is a definite trend toward nationality self-assertion in Soviet Moldavia, although the new intellectuals seem to be very careful not to be accused of Romanian irredentism. Furthermore, the new generation of young writers is more outspoken. A young poet writes with pride of his love for Moldavia and an established novelist makes one of his characters say that she wants her children to have Moldavian names, and gives as examples the most common Romanian ones.[33]

Increasingly, Moldavian names appear among writers, theater people, movie producers and even in the Moldavian Academy.

Publications of the last few years include a Moldavian encyclopedic dictionary, Latin grammars, direct translations from the French, and the first Moldavian linguistic atlas, based not only on fieldwork in the Moldavian villages of the MSSR and the Ukraine, but also in three villages in the Northern Caucasus, three in Central Asia, two in the Omsk region of West Siberia, and eight in the Far East.[34] Buried in the back of a recent issue of <u>Nistru</u> is a reproduction of a book cover on the Romanian author Eminescu, printed in Latin characters in Bucharest.[35] There is a new generation preoccupied with new problems; there are likewise new problems for the Soviet regime.

Thus, based upon research in the fields of linguistics, literature, folk art, history, and social attitudes one can conclude that there is no distinctive Moldavian nationality. The real nationality identification of the indigenous population of Moldavia is Romanian, though this is not, of course, explicitly stated in the Soviet press. The so-called Moldavian nationality was advanced by the Soviet authorities as a justification of the annexation of the former Romanian province. It is therefore contended here that problems stemming from the contradiction between the reality of nationality identity and its official Soviet representation are to be expected to an even greater degree in the future.

It appears from evidence available in the local Moldavian press that the young intellectuals have struggled for many years to impose a literary language and nationality recognition from within, although to date only as "Moldavian" and not Romanian. Along the same lines, a strong Romanian influence is exerted upon Moldavians through external channels, including the recently-built radio and television stations at Iaşi, near the Soviet border, which cover all of Soviet Moldavia with Romanian programs.[36] With growing national ferment from within, and Romanian influence from without, the question arises: How successful can the Soviet authorities be in convincing Moldavians that they are a separate nationality?

Soviet attempts to foster a new Moldavian nationality are in conflict with reality, and to date have apparently been a failure. A British writer who has recently published a book on Romania has concluded: 'The superior power of the Soviet Union guarantees that the people of the Moldavian SSR and of the other areas which once were Romanian, will remain Soviet citizens for a long time to come. But they will never be anything but Romanian."[37]

APPENDIX: MOLDAVIAN OR ROMANIAN?
A LINGUISTIC CONTENT ANALYSIS

The following sentence which, freely translated, means

In the true sense of the word, political power is the
power organized by one class for the purpose of sub-
jugating another class

is given below in the standard language of the Socialist Republic of
Romania (1) and in four Moldavian versions (2 to 5) from the years
indicated. A literal translation is provided for the first version; the
reader is invited to compare the other versions with it. Where these
other versions differ from the first one, literal translations are again
provided. See also the comments which follow the sample.

1. Standard Bucharest Romanian
    In sensul   propriu al   cuvíntului, puterea   politică
    in sense-the proper of-the word's   power-the political
    este puterea   organizată a unei clase
    is   power-the organized of a   class's
    pentru   asuprirea   alteia.
    for(-the-purpose-of) domination-the another's
2. Moldavian, 1948.
    Puterea politica în înțelesul propriu al cuvîntului —aiasta-i
                      meaning   this is
    silnicia   organizată a unei clase, pentru înăbușirea   alteia.
    effort-the   suffocation-the
3. Moldavian, 1953.
    Puterea politică în înțelesul propriu al cuvîntului îi silnicia
                                                        is
    organizată a unei clase pentru asuprirea alteia.
4. Moldavian, 1961.
    Puterea politică, în înțelesul propriu al cuvîntului, este forța
                                                              force-the
    organizată a unei clase pentru asuprirea alteia.
5. Moldavian, 1972.
    In sensul propriu al cuvîntului, puterea politică este violența
                                                             violence-the
    organizată a unei clase pentru reprimarea   alteia.
                                   repression-the
    We encounter the following variables:

1	2	3	4	5	Com-ments
sensul	înțelesul	înțelesul	înțelesul	sensul	(a)
- - -	aiasta	- - - - - - - - -	- - -	(b)

	1	2	3	4	5	Comments
	este	-i	îi	este	este	(c)
	puterea	silnicia	silnicia	forţa	violenţa	(d)
	asuprirea	înăbusirea	asuprirea	asuprirea	reprimarea	(e)

(a) Sens(ul) is a neologism, based on French; înţeles(ul) is a native formation (Rom. înţeleg 'I understand'). -ul is the masc. article.

(b) Aiasta 'this (thing)', fem. demonstr. article, occurs only in 2. It introduces the predicate (cf. Russian X, èto Y 'X, this is Y', in the meaning of 'X is Y'). This is an obvious Slavicism. This construction can occur in any dialect, but is used mostly for folksy or rhetorical effect. The form itself is dialectal.

(c) The word for 'is' has many forms. All those listed here can also occur in the standard, but este is the normal one in this (official) context; the others are conversational or affected.

(d) The Moldavian forms in 4 and 5 are, interestingly enough, the ones based on West European models; silnicia is from Slavic; puterea is a native formation from the verb 'to be able to'.

(e) Similarly, asuprirea (1, 3, 4) is a native formation (cf. asupra 'upon'), reprimarea is West European, and înăbuşire is native.

It seems obvious that between 1948 and 1972, the trend in the MSSR has been away from a Slavicizing influence and toward a more hospitable acceptance of West European models.

NOTES

1. Hedrick Smith, "Moldavia Pioneering Factories on the Farm," New York Times, November 4, 1971, p. 14.

2. Andrei Popovici, The Political Status of Bessarabia (Washington: Ransdell, 1931), p. 14.

3. Stefan Ciobanu, La Bessarabie (Bucharest: Academie Roumaine, 1941), pp. 39-40.

4. Karl Marx, Notes on Romanians (Bucharest: Editura Academiei, 1964), pp. 105-06.

5. Julian Hale, Ceausescu's Rumania (London: George Herrop & Co., 1971), p. 183.

6. Outline History of the USSR (Moscow: Foreign Languages Publishing House, 1960), p. 122.

7. A. L. Odud, R. S. S. Moldovenească (Kishinev: EDS a Moldovei, 1957), p. 62.

8. P. Cazacu, Moldova dintre Prut şi Nistru (Iaşi: Viaţa Românească, 1920), pp. 146-49.

9. Pervaia vseobshchaia perepis naseleniia Rossiskogo Imperii 1897 (Petersburg: Tsentral'ninii Statisticheskiy Komitet, 1905). Bessarabia Volume.

10. F. Aftenivc, Moldova Socialistă, December 15, 1972, p. 3.

11. J. Dobândă, "Calea grandioaselor Transformări pe Pămîntul Moldovenesc," Nistru, August 1972, pp. 81-90.

12. J. Bodiul, "Starea educării marxist-leniniste a oamenilor muncii din Republică," Cultura, No. 2 (January 1966), pp. 2-7.

13. Hedrick Smith, "Soviet is Loosening Moldavia-Rumania Ties," New York Times, November 6, 1971.

14. V. Zelenchuk, "Cu privire la Particularitățile caracteristice ale comunității etnice Moldovenești," Comunistul Moldovei, October 1972, pp. 29-36.

15. Moldova Socialistă, August 13, 1972.

16. V. Zelenchuk, pp. 29-36.

17. Jon Dumitru, Forme de etnocid in URSS (Munich: Editura Avdella-Cenad, 1969), pp. 24-25.

18. "In marea verde a taigei," Moldova Socialistă, April 27, 1969.

19. Moldova Socialistă, January 27, 1973, p. 4.

20. J. Bodiul, pp. 2-7.

21. V. V. Pokshishevskiy, "On Basic Migration Patterns," in Population Geography: A Reader, ed. George J. Demko, Harold M. Rose, and George A. Schnell (New York: McGraw-Hill, 1970), pp. 321-27.

22. Clifton R. Wharton, Jr., "The Green Revolution," Foreign Affairs, 47, No. 3, (1969), p. 475.

23. T. H. Rigby, Communist Party Membership in the Soviet Union (Princeton: Princeton University Press, 1968), p. 378.

24. ATEM, "Republica în vesmînt de Sărbătoare," Tinerimea Moldovei, November 10, 1972, p. 3.

25. Who's Who 1972-1973 (New York: St. Martin's Press, 1972), p. 370.

26. ATEM "Congresul 4 al Societății teatrale din Moldova," Cultura, No. 4 (January 1973), p. 2.

27. N. Gubareva, "Totalurile unei Conferințe," Cultura, No. 481 (December 1972), p. 4.

28. Vernon V. Aspaturian, "The Non-Russian Nationalities," in Prospects for Soviet Society, Allen Kassof (New York: Praeger, 1968), P. 167.

29. A. Lunacharskii, "Câteva Probleme de Terminologie," Cultura, No. 48 (December 1972), pp. 6-7.

30. Vasile Badiul, "Ion Creangă, Opere," Cultura, No. 4 (January 1973), p. 4.

31. Moldova Socialistă, January 12, 1973, p. 2.

32. G. Ceaicovski, "500 Melodii," Cultura, No. 6 (February 1973), p. 7.

33. A. Busuioc, "Unchiul din Paris," Nistru, August 1972, pp. 44-80.

34. <u>Cultura</u>, No. 16 (July 1965).
35. Cărți Noi, <u>Nistru</u>, August 1972, p. 158.
36. Nicolae Dima, "Despre Basarabia," <u>America Romanian News</u>, September 1971, p. 10.
37. Julian Hale, pp. 186-87.

4

THE THEORETICAL BASIS
FOR THE DEFINITION OF
MOLDAVIAN NATIONALITY

Walter Feldman

Given the irredentist nature of the Moldavian population inhabiting the area known today as the Moldavian Soviet Socialist Republic (MSSR), it is not surprising that Soviet authorities have frequently stressed the distinctiveness of the Moldavians vis-à-vis the Romanians. There are, however, a number of theoretical positions upon which such a distinctiveness could conceivably be based. The purpose of this paper will be to examine briefly the historical background of Moldavia, and, from the cultural and demographic history of the region, to propose several hypothetical positions upon which a Moldavian identity might be justified. These theoretical positions for a distinct Moldavian identity will be examined through the utilization of current press and literary materials from Soviet Moldavia in an attempt to identify the position actually advocated by Soviet authorities.

The principal sources employed in this study were the following Moldavian-language newspapers and journals: Moldova Socialistă (daily), July 1972 through February 1973; Cultura (weekly), July through November 1972, and January through February 1973; Comunistul Moldovei (monthly), July 1972 through February 1973; Tinerimea Moldovei (a semiweekly), January through February 1973; and Nistru (monthly), July through November 1972. The first three are Communist party publications, whereas the first of the last pair is a Komsomol paper and the second is a publication of the Writers' Union. Additional works about history and folklore were also consulted.

Evidence sought in these sources varied according to the type of information contained in them. After the format and general contents of all the publications were surveyed, explicit references to nationality were noted, both in connection with the titular nationality and ethnic minorities, and then for references to neighboring Soviet republics and the Romanian Socialist Republic. References to urban culture (literature, and so on), to folklore, and especially to the performing groups (which is the form in which references to folklore tend to appear in nonscholarly publications), were noted. These references to performing groups and folklore were of particular importance because they provided most of the rare references to ethnic minorities and because the content of their repertoires could be useful as a partial indicator of the official attitude toward ethnic identity. Publications of the Ethnographic Section of the Moldavian Academy of Sciences were not available. Historical articles were of great value, not so much for specific information but rather as indicators of current attitudes. These viewpoints were occasionally expounded at length, but, more typically, were simply assumed by the writers of the articles and had to be deduced from both the positive and negative evidence found in them.

The concept of a distinct Moldavian identity is promulgated by the government of the MSSR, the Communist party of the MSSR, and all cultural organizations. Among these organizations, the ones whose expressions are most accessible and pertinent to this inquiry (because of the nature of available research sources) are the Writers' Union and Ministry of Culture as well as the various professional and amateur folklore-performing ensembles which function under its aegis. No doubt educational institutions must be involved as well, but explicit evidence of their participation in this identification of Moldavian nationality has not been sought in the sources.[1] However, writings by individuals connected with academic institutions suggest that these institutions are involved as well.

Because of the fundamental character of nationality identity, the sectors of society which official theorizing is designed to reach via the cultural apparatus is very wide—in fact the whole of the titular nationality of the Moldavian Republic. Thus the current theory of nationality identity is not primarily connected with any subdivision of the nationality either on Party, occupational, residential, or age lines, although it must be directed along these channels. It is the Moldavian-speaking population which is primarily involved. Ethnic minorities within the MSSR, such as the Ukrainians, Jews, and Bulgarians, do not play an active role in defining the official titular nationality, although as individuals all citizens of the Republic must be aware of the trend of official thinking.

Moldavia forms a part of the Soviet West, which for present purposes also includes Estonia, Lithuania, Latvia, the Ukraine, and Belorussia. Its proximity of Romania, a non-Soviet state with which it shares strong ethnic, cultural, and historical ties, however, renders its situation somewhat different from most of the others. Nationality consciousness (asserted nationality identity) cannot be considered apart from subjective group identity, or self-image, which is

47

vulnerable to direct and indirect influences from official pressures. Unlike the concept "nationality" which involves a set of criteria imposed by an outside observer, "nationality consciousness" is a subjective attitude of the group itself. In a global and historical perspective, this term may have a variety of nuances, but here we will employ it to designate that form of group awareness connected with ethnicity and a nation-state which characterizes the peoples of Western Europe.

Roughly speaking, the Moldavian Soviet Socialist Republic comprises the territory lying between the River Prut in the west, and the Dnestr (Nistru) in the east. This area, together with some additional territory to the north and south had comprised both the Czarist and Romanian provinces of Bessarabia (Map 2). On the right bank of the Prut (outside the MSSR) lie four administrative regions of the Romanian Socialist Republic (Suceava, Bacau, Iaşi and Galati) which are collectively, in historical and ethnographic connections, referred to as Moldavia. The Suceava region is sometimes popularly called (Southern) Bukovina; it lies just south of Chernovtsy Oblast of the Ukrainian SSR, which is likewise popularly called Bukovina, or Northern Bukovina.[2] In addition, in 1924 the Soviet government had established a Moldavian Republic centered around the town of Balta, east of the Dnestr, in a territory with a compact Moldavian population. This area has in the past been referred to as "Transdniestria." Today the majority of this smaller territory forms part of Vinnitsa and Odessa Oblasts of the Ukraine; only a small portion is included in the contemporary MSSR (See Map 2.)

The Moldavian regions of the present Romanian Socialist Republic will be referred to here as Western Moldavia, whereas the present-day territory of Soviet Moldavia will be referred to as the MSSR. The general area of both the past and present will be termed Bessarabia. For convenience, both the written and spoken language of the MSSR will be described as "Moldavian" without implying anything about its connection to the spoken language of Western Moldavia or to literary Romanian. Likewise the titular nationality of the MSSR will be called the "Moldavians" for the present and the "Bessarabians" for past epochs. The most convenient term to distinguish all speakers of Danubian Balkan-Romance (Daco-Romanian) is "Romanian," which will be used here.

In publications of the MSSR, all historical, cultural, and linguistic phenomena pertaining to the titular nationality are described as "Moldavian." Beneath this blanket terminology, however, lies the real problem of defining and orienting the "Moldavian" population. The purpose of this study is to help clarify the thinking behind the Soviet phraseology in relation to Moldavia. The question is: How do the Soviets justify the existence of a Moldavian SSR and who, in nationality terms, are the "Moldavians"? Can a region or province

sustain the weight of independent national existence, particularly
when there is an urban intelligentsia involved who view things in
larger than regional terms? Since, as will be shown, the Soviets
insist upon the separate identify of the "Moldavian" nationality, on
what basis do they differentiate it from the Romanian nation?

The existence of the (Bessarabian) Moldavians as the titular
nationality of a Soviet republic does not mean that the Soviets take
the MSSR to be the only area with a significant concentration of
Moldavian population. The formation of a Soviet republic out of a
section of a larger ethnic area is not a pattern unique in the Soviet
West, but has occurred elsewhere in the USSR, for instance in Azerbaijan. Nevertheless, neither the people nor the authorities of the
Azerbaijan SSR consider the Soviet Azeri Turks to be a nationality
separate from the Azeris of Iran or the smaller communities in Turkey. If it can be assumed that the Soviet ideologists feel obliged to
substantiate their contention that a Moldavian nationality indeed exists
(and is not an ad hoc creation with no historical foundation), three
possible bases may support that identification. Briefly, the first
would create a Moldavian nationality restricted to Bessarabia, the
second would posit a supraethnic Bessarabian nationality based solely
on the region, while the third would treat the populations of both the
MSSR and Romanian Moldavia together as a Moldavian nationality.
These three hypothetical bases for Moldavian national identity will
be discussed at length further on.

Today the observer is confronted with the appearance of two
Moldavias, one a regional designation and part of the Romanian
Socialist Republic, and the other a Soviet republic. Within Soviet
Moldavia the Moldavians constitute a solid majority, being a rural,
agricultural people with a high fertility rate, thus enabling them to
counteract in numbers (at least for the time being) the increasing
in-migration of Russians and Ukrainians. Excluding the languages
used in minority (Gagauz, Ukrainian) and Russian publications, the
written language of the Republic is described as "Moldavian" and is
printed in Cyrillic characters. Even slight acquaintance with the
"Moldavian" language reveals it to be essentially literary Romanian,
with a minimum of neologisms. These neologisms are more often
formed from native roots or from French than from Russian. Before
the mid-1950s Russianisms and regional vocabulary were common,
but neither is much in evidence today.

At the time of the 1970 Soviet census the Moldavians numbered
2,304,000 out of the total Republic population of 3,569,000.[3] The
largest ethnic minority of the Republic is the Ukrainian, given as
507,000 in 1970. However, the Ukrainians enumerated in the census
consist, in fact, of two distinct groups: 1) the Ukrainians proper or
East Ukrainians, who are found mainly in the southern part of the

49

Republic (besides Kishinev, the capital) and in the Yedenits and other northern raions, and 2) the Ruthenians (also Rusniaks, Carpatho-Ukrainians, Carpatho-Russians, or less properly, Huțuli or Gutsuls) who live almost solely in the northern raions.[4] The Ruthenians of the MSSR are predominantly of the same dialect branch as those living in the Chernovtsy Oblast of the Ukraine and the Suceava region of Romania (where they are named Huțuli, and sometimes refer to themselves as Bukovintsy).

The old settlements of heterodox Russians formerly in the Czarist province of Bessarabia are now in Odessa Oblast of the Ukraine, so that they are absent from the 1970 census figure of 414,000 for the Russians of the MSSR. The Eastern Orthodox Gagauz, speakers of an Oghuz Turkic language closely related to Osman, number 125,000; the Jews 98,000; and the Bulgarians 74,000. The smaller groups, including the Armenians, Greeks, and Gypsies total 47,000.

The origins of the present-day Moldavian speaking population of the MSSR are to be found in the fourteenth century, when Bessarabia began to receive settlers from the Moldavian Principality, which was centered on the west bank of the Prut. By the beginning of the fifteenth century much of the land fell under the control of the Moldavian princes.[5]

The Wallachian and Moldavian Principalities remained the only political organizations of the Romanians until both came under the control of the Osman Turks (Wallachia in 1476, Moldavia in 1511). The degree of autonomy allowed Moldavia by the Turks was very great; her princely line remained intact and she retained control over Bessarabia as a part of Moldavia. In the early nineteenth century, Turkey, under heavy Russian pressure, ceded all of Bessarabia to the Czar, a move which was illegal according to the provisions of the sixteenth-century treaty of Bogdan II, which assured the territorial integrity of Moldavia.[6] Thereafter (except for a brief period following the Crimean War, in which southern Bessarabia was given to the new state of Romania), Bessarabia (in 1812) became a province of Russia. In 1775, the Porte had granted a smaller piece of Moldavia, the so-called Bukovina (including the ancient Moldavian capital, Suceava) to Austria.

The nineteenth century saw a significant development in Western Moldavia, for in 1858 the Moldavian prince, Alexandru Cuza, was elected to the thrones of both Moldavia and Wallachia. The election of Cuza created for the first time a durable political structure covering both regions, which continues today, with additions, as the state of Romania. The Bessarabians of course had no share in this political move and remained under Russian rule (except for the brief transfer of Southern Bessarabia to Romania) until 1919, when they were annexed by Romania. The recent history is well known. The Romanian government over Bessarabia was removed in 1940 by the Soviets, but was soon reestablished with the aid of the Germans. The end of the Second World War brought with it the end of the Romanian regime in the area and the reincorporation of Bessarabia into the Soviet Union, this time as the MSSR.

The history of Bessarabia and its present-day demography supply the material from which the three possible bases already mentioned for Moldavian national identity may be inferred. The first possibility revolves around the year 1812 when the Bessarabians fell under Czarist rule. This change in political regime had profound effects on the entire population, for the Russians pursued a policy of active linguistic and cultural Russification. The Bessarabians were then an almost totally rural group, so that only one of their cultural institutions, the church, existed beyond the village level. Russian attacks on the Moldavian Orthodox Church, which grew in intensity from the 1870s onward, caused a real break in Moldavian cultural life, as the forced Russification of the Church deprived the peasantry of their one spiritual, cultural, and educational institution. By the end of the nineteenth and into the early twentieth century, the near-total illiteracy of the ordinary Bessarabians and their alienation from organized religion was alarming even to the Russian ecclesiastical hierarchy.[7] The growth of Kishinev (Chisinau) into a large urban center brought no benefits to the Moldavians, because it was an almost entirely Russian and Jewish city which disseminated Russian culture. In addition, the Russian economy was responsible for various changes in village life, including the virtual destruction of home crafts which are alive to this day in Western Moldavia.[8] All this, added to the already existing topographical and related economic differences between the two Moldavian regions (such as significant pastoralism in the West, as opposed to almost exclusive agriculture in the East), as well as to the fact that Bessarabia had no part in the nineteenth-century political and cultural developments certainly could suggest the basis for a separate Bessarabian or "Soviet Moldavian" nationality.

However, the Moldavian sources supporting this study do not express that view. Both historical and cultural references treat the Moldavian heritage on both sides of the Prut as a continuum, both before and after 1812. From the point of view of the Moldavian intelligentsia, the creation of a Moldavian nationality of Bessarabia would cut them off from the rich Moldavo-Romanian cultural life of the last century and would render them completely dependent upon the Russians in the cultural sphere.

A second possible basis for Moldavian identity would center around regional identification. This approach would have the advantage of dealing positively with the minorities. In this hypothetical interpretation "Moldavian" would acquire a purely spatial or regional meaning and would include the entire population of the Republic, regardless of language or religious background. In the case of Moldavia such a position would have a degree of historical validity because many of the older minority communities have undergone total or partial assimilation to the Moldavians. The landed Ruthenian population of the north has indeed formed the basis for much of the "Moldavian" peasantry of the area, for many villagers still preserve their Ruthenian family names as the last vestige of their ancestors' nationality.[9] A similar situation exists in parts of Chernovtsy Oblast of the Ukraine and in the Suceava region of Romania where the Ruthenian-speakers (called Huţuli in Romania) have lost almost every feature of their original costume, music, dance, and the like, and have adopted Moldavian forms.[10]

One group in the MSSR, the Ashkenazic Jews, might prove amenable to such a theoretical position, because it does, to a certain degree, depict their situation. The Ashkenazic Jews in semirural situations do have a high rate of regional identification in Moldavia, as they do elsewhere, since so many of their cultural and folkloric traits are always local and not specifically their own. More than any other minority in the region, their closest contact has always been with the Moldavians, particularly in rural areas, as seen in their Yiddish dialect, music, and other folk-cultural manifestations. Their political and urban-cultural orientation has long been Russian, but the increased urbanization of the Moldavian Jews since the Second World War has also brought them into contact with a newly urbanized Moldavian Christian population.

The regional basis for a Moldavian identity, however, rests on a rather static and older stage of Moldavian demography, for it does not take into account the recent large in-migration of Russians and Ukrainians who have no long-standing ties with the Moldavian land or its people. Another problem is posed by the smaller minorities to the south. These have mixed less with the Moldavians and live in close proximity to other communities of their own ethnic groups located in other Soviet republics or in other countries (the Bulgarians and Gagauz of Bulgaria, Romania, and the Ukrainian SSR).

A further proof of the continued separateness of the ethnic groups, both in fact and in official thinking, is provided by the folk ensembles, some of which perform not only "Moldavian, but Russian, Ukrainian, Gagauz, and Bulgarian folklore as well."[11] It is clear from this terminology that the Moldavians are a nationality like the Ukrainians, Gagauz and others. Kishinev school children are pictured on one occasion in "national costume" which happens to be Ukrainian. It is also clear that the repertoires of the groups display no overt merging of the nationalities. In the state ensemble, "Zhok," the artistic approach shows no major incorporation of foreign or local non-Moldavian minority elements except for one rather arbitrary alteration of the male costume for some of the dances. In fact, the most striking instance of such incorporation involves non-Moldavian, Romanian material. Most notable is the spectacular ritual dance of the Calusari, which has been dead for a long time in both Moldavias, if indeed it ever existed there at all, but which is performed by "Zhok" in the style of Oltenia (Southwest Romania) where the custom does exist.[12]

Finally, a policy of nationality identification based on Soviet Moldavia as a region is at odds with the concept of the USSR as a federation of nationalities organized within titular republics. On a cultural level, such a policy would prove unsatisfactory for the same reason the preceding theory did—estrangement from past west Moldavian culture and history. Further, the policy of a regional rather than Moldavian ethnic identity would render totally illogical the sporadic references to west Moldavian culture and history which do occur in publications of the MSSR.

Only one further possibility for a Moldavian identity remains, namely that the Moldavians of the MSSR do not form an ethnic unit but that all Moldavians, east and west, do, and did form one, at least since the thirteenth century. Leninist thought puts much emphasis upon language as part of the makeup of any nationality, but this aspect of the Moldavian nationality question is not being viewed by Soviet ideologues as primary. The Bessarabian spoken language is certainly not unintelligible to Romanian-speakers and is less distinctive than some of the dialects of western Romania. With language as a neutral factor, where can one look for the special traits of the contemporary "Moldavian nation"?

A Soviet view of this question is put forth in a recent Comunistul Moldovei article entitled "Regarding the Characteristic Peculiarities of Moldavian Ethnic Communities," written by a local historian.[13] He presents the medieval history of the Moldavians briefly, describing the settlement of Bessarabia and emphasizing the complete political and cultural separation of the two Romance-speaking principalities; the Moldavians and Wallachians are represented as two ethnic groups, and pains are taken to demonstrate their appearance as such in medieval documents. The ethnic link between the Wallachians and the Moldavians is never denied outright, however, and the larger prenational formation out of which both arose is termed "Romance" (Romanik) and is expressly distinguished from "Romanian" (roman), which term, the author states, was never employed by Moldavians prior to the creation of the Romanian state. He then attacks the "bourgeois" historical notion that this distinction was solely political, without ethnic implications. In the course of his critique, the historian briefly mentions aspects of culture peculiar to the Moldavians, such as architectural styles and the well known carpet-weaving and embroidering tradition of Moldavia (which was, incidentally, most characteristic of Bessarabia). He ascribes much of the distinctiveness of Moldavian folk-production to prolonged contact with East Slavic and Oriental people.

Among the sources consulted for this study, the above contains the clearest expression of current Soviet nationality theory with regard to the Moldavians. The argument put forth there renders all other references found in recent Soviet material absolutely coherent and consistent. It certainly appears, therefore, that of the three hypothetical policies upon which a Moldavian nationality identity might be based, the Soviet emphasis is to stress an identity that transcends regions and international borders to foster a Moldavian identity that includes Soviet as well as Romanian Moldavia.

In addition to nationality theory, the sources supply some information about actual policy toward the Moldavian nationality and an example of how nationality policy is directed along social group lines. Evidence from the late 1960s and from the early 1970s points to sharp attacks on village folklore by Soviet officials within the MSSR and in Moldavian villages in the Ukraine.

In 1965 and 1966 Sunday dances (hora) were banned in villages in the northern Yedenits raion, and in some cases the instruments of the local musicians were confiscated.[14] The New Year's ceremony, a folkloric survival of older magico-religious ceremonies, is characteristic of the northern Carpathian populations of various nationalities and although it is only peripherally connected with church ceremonies that take place at the same season, it was prohibited to children.[15] Similar customs were banned in some of the socialist countries in the 1950s. The seasonal celebrations are rich sources of specialized song, dance, folk-poetry and art, and their prohibition to the young will almost certainly condemn all of these customs to oblivion. Without distinctive linguistic identity the weakening or forced demise of village cultural expression would ultimately have a detrimental effect on the vitality of the nationality culture, given the largely rural situation of the Moldavian population. In a different economic environment, urban stage "folklore," together with the creation of a new urban folklore or culture, can satisfy different emotional needs. This has not occurred yet in Moldavia; therefore, rural folklore does play a role, perhaps indirectly, in the maintenance of nationality consciousness. Thus the suppression of village folklore can constitute unpropitious conditions for such vitality.

Official moves initiated against village cultural expression, no doubt, furnish part of the background for a revealing interview published recently in which a member of the Writers' Union assailed the Artistic Director of the Republican Ensemble "Zhok" for "taking creativity away from its rightful owners, the whole people." The critic accused the director of achieving this by manufacturing inauthentic steps and choreographies and overly orchestrating the folk music.[16]

Together with the policy of Moldavian distinctiveness, there appears to be a concurrent effort by the Soviet government to pursue the estrangement of the MSSR from Romania in general, on both a theoretical and emotional level. One aspect of the relationship of the MSSR to Romania is the largely negative memories held by the Bessarabians dating back to the time of the interwar Romanian government and the wartime fascist occupation. In Moldavian publications both of these periods are treated extremely negatively. The "occupation of the Romanian boyars"[17] is described as a "sad period" in the history of Moldavia, and the Communist-led guerrilla operations at the close of World War I and in the 1920s are frequently recalled. The defense of Bender (against the post-World War I Romanian occupation army) and the "Tatar Bunar Incident" (a Communist-led uprising against the Romanian administration) are frequently mentioned.[18] The defense of Bender is described as a "fight against reactionary elements led by bourgeois nationalists."[19]

Certain of the more onerous aspects of the Romanian period have become cliches, not only in the MSSR, but in the Ukraine as well. For example, mention of a mode of punishment and discipline used in the Romanian army appeared in the Moldavian press[20] and in a recent film shot in Chernovtsy Oblast.[21] The Romanian occupation of Transnistria (Transdniestria) is, of course, severely attacked, and the World War II Romanian leader Antonescu's remarks about Romanianizing this area is compared to Hitler's statements about Germanizing the East.[22]

The contemporary Romanian Socialist Republic is not the target of attacks in Moldavian publications, but neither is it a subject of notice. This silence is quite striking. In the sources covered, only one mention of contact with Romania, a brief notice about a visiting delegation, and only one publication notice from Bucharest were discovered.[23]

Crucial in the Moldavian relationship to Romania is the question of Western Moldavia. Because this region's kinship with the MSSR has been amply demonstrated by Soviet spokesmen, its existence separate from the MSSR must appear anomalous. Although such thoughts are expressed only theoretically in the writings, their practical potential is certainly evident. If, in the Soviet view, the proper place for the Moldavians lies within the USSR, why should they be sundered from their brethren across the Prut, thus dividing one "nation"?

The question of Moldavian nationality and nationality consciousness cannot be considered separately from the identity of the other
Romanian-speakers. Today the majority of the Romanian population
lives within the Romanian Socialist Republic and either possesses
or is presently developing a Romanian nationality consciousness.
There are, however, a few small communities of the same Daco-
Romanian language group who are not now and never were governed
as part of a Romanian political state. Such a group is that of the
Timok valley in East Serbia (Yugoslavia) who are no more culturally
differentiated from the people of Romania than are the Moldavians
of the MSSR. Nevertheless, their self-identity remains on an ethno-
linguistic level (as Vlakhs), and on a regional level, but it does not
reflect Romanian nationality consciousness.

The nationality identity of the Moldavians must also be considered
from the economic and class point of view. The Moldavians are an
overwhelmingly rural, agricultural people, and as settled peasants
their local identification is strong. The 1970 Soviet census enumerated
only 20.4 percent of the Moldavians as urban dwellers, whereas the
USSR average was 56.3 percent urban.[24] The rise of an urban intelligentsia of Moldavian, as opposed to Russian or Jewish, origin within
Bessarabia is mainly a recent, largely post-World War II phenomenon;
the center of Moldavian cultural development lay in Western Moldavia.
Thus the needs and self-images of the rural and urban populations
of the MSSR may well differ somewhat, but both must be taken into
account by the Soviet leaders.

Perhaps the most important aspect of Soviet nationality policy
in the MSSR is the degree of acceptance which the official nationality
identification will win among the Moldavians. Answers to this question can only be hinted at in the present study. Likewise, the historical
validity of the Soviet position has not been discussed at length. Certain points should, however, be mentioned which may be useful in
treating both of these topics.

Moldavia as a whole differs from other Romanian-speaking
regions because it alone experienced an independent political development parallel to that of Wallachia. Bessarabia differs from West
Moldavia politically. West Moldavia was part of the Moldavian Principality until 1858, and has been an integral part of the Romanian
state for the last 115 years, whereas Bessarabia experienced Romanian rule for only 21 years (1919-1940). Bessarabia was separated
from the Moldavian Principality over 160 years ago.

The Bessarabians, nevertheless, share a great many cultural
traits with other Romanian-speakers. Certain of these traits may
prove to be in tension with Soviet nationality policy. The Romanians
(including the Moldavians) constitute a group conserving elements
of an earlier historical experience. Their very existence as a

linguistic and ethnic community is evidence of this conservatism. Historically, they have been unaware of or cut off from any other group with whom they could identify in linguistic and ethnic terms. They were, of course, aware of the Slavic and Magyar speaking groups which surrounded them, and thus an important basis of Romano-Moldavian self-identification was a negative one. Their earliest history was characterized by physical isolation due to their pastoral and high altitude economy, and their recent history shows much evidence of their continued assimilation of alien groups. This negative self-identification has given the Romano-Moldavians a noticeable cultural unity which worked against the centrifugal forces of regionalism and foreign domination. It is precisely this socially agglutinative quality of the Romano-Moldavians which the Soviets are combatting in their redefinition of the Moldavian nationality.

In the Soviet West a basic distinction should be made between those groups that have developed a nationality consciousness comparable to the nationalities of the West, and those among whom this process has begun only recently and is presently being guided by Leninist doctrine and Soviet policy. The Baltic nationalities fall into the first category and the Belorussians and Ruthenians into the second.

The Baltic people, despite a lack of political independence during most of their modern history, have strong linguistic, cultural and religious traits separating them from their neighbors, their past and present rulers, and from each other. In addition, in the Middle Ages they had already experienced a separate development which provided a basis for cohesion in each group continuing to the modern period. Furthermore, prolonged Baltic contact with such West European groups as the Germans, Swedes, and Danes is a factor to be considered as well in Latvian and Estonian nationality integrity.

At the other extreme stand the Belorussians, physically and culturally wedged in between the Russians and the Poles. The Belorussians provide the closest analogy to the Moldavians in the Soviet West, for they are considered by Soviet authorities to be at a stage wherein regional distinctiveness can bear the weight of nationality, although in the Belorussian case the experience of political autonomy in any period is absent.

The modern period of Ukrainian nationality development and consciousness began in the seventeenth century, but this mainly involved the Eastern Ukraine. The so-called Western Ukraine, especially the Carpathian region, is the home of various East Slavic groups whose self-identification was essentially regional (Hutsuls, Lemko, and others). The Ukrainians thus represent a situation opposite from that of the Belorussians and Moldavians, because they are composed of two peoples (the Ukrainians and Ruthenians) who have been joined despite the linguistic, religious, economic, historical and folkloristic barriers which separated them.

Moldavia differs from much of the rest of the Soviet West, for in the MSSR the Soviet authorities are apparently attempting to foster nationality identity and vitality, but along Soviet lines and according to Soviet definitions. A Moldavian nationality consciousness is evidently held by them to be less divisive than a nationality consciousness identified with a non-Soviet state. This fostering of Moldavian nationality consciousness, if successful, can strengthen the Soviet position among the Moldavians, who may come to accept a nationality identity which is recognized only within the USSR.

NOTES

C. - Cultura; C.M. - Comunistul Moldovei; M.S. - Moldova Socialistă; N. - Nistru.

1. V. Zelenchuk, "Ku privire la partikularitetsile karakteristiche ale Komunitetsii etniche moldoveneshti," C.M., No. 10, October 1972, p. 29.

2. "Pe meliagurile Bukovinei," M.S., September 17, 1972, p. 3.

3. These and following figures from "Naselenie nashei strany," Pravda, April 17, 1971, p. 3.

4. C.U. Clark, Bessarabia (New York: Dodd, Mead, 1927), p. 62.

5. A. Popovici, The Political Status of Bessarabia (Washington, D.C.: Georgetown University, 1931), p. 39.

6. Ibid.

7. Clark, p. 108.

8. Ibid.

9. Ibid., p. 62.

10. T. Banateanu, et al., Folk Costumes (Bucharest, 1958), no page numbers (under "Hutzuli").

11. "Mioritsa yn Italia," M.S., September 24, 1972, p. 4.

12. T. Alexandru, The Folk Music of Rumania (Columbia World Library of Folk and Primitive Music), Vol. XVII, side 2, band 2.

13. Zelenchuk, p. 29.

14. I. Dimitru, Forme de Etnocid in URSS (Munchen: Lutai, 1969), pp. 63-64.

15. Ibid.

16. "Interviul Nostru," N. No. 7, July 1972, p. 104.

17. I. Bodiul, "Roadele marii fretsii a popoarelor," M.S., July 18, 1972, p. 104.

18. Clark, pp. 261-76.

19. A. Zaichev, "Nesupenere," M.S., February 7, 1973, p. 4.

20. D. Voiturin "Iosif Buzhor—militant ynflekerat pentry kauza norodului," N. No. 10, October 1972, p. 146.

21. M.Y. Ilenko, "White Bird with Black Spot."

22. M. Muntean, "Sub maska obiektivitetsii," C., November 25, 1972, p. 12.

23. "Oaspetsi din Romynia," M.S., February 1, 1973, p. 4.

24. Itogi vsesoiuznoi perepisi naseleniia 1970 goda. (Moscow: Statistika, 1973), IV, 27.

5

THE INTEGRATION OF UKRAINIANS INTO MODERNIZED SOCIETY IN THE UKRAINIAN SSR
Ralph S. Clem

By integrating various nationalities of the Soviet West into the advanced urban work force via the process of modernization (here defined as industrialization, urbanization, and higher educational levels), the Soviet government seemingly attempts to counter the individuality of these nationalities in order to facilitate their incorporation into an ethnically undifferentiated state. Socioeconomic forces, both directly and indirectly controlled by the Soviet government, affect this integration. This study focuses on the integration of Ukrainians into the advanced sectors of society in the Ukrainian SSR, but the generalizations detailed here no doubt apply to other republics of the Soviet West.

The methodology utilized in this chapter is that of the interdisciplinary group in general: the description and analysis of the interplay between nationality and identifiable social, economic, or political sectors of the population. In this instance, interest centers on the interaction of the largest nationality of the Soviet West, the Ukrainians, with a social and economic sector to be called the advanced urban work force. Also, the participation of Russians in this same advanced work force will be examined because of their obvious importance, and brief mention will be made of the role of Belorussians and Jews. Although there is no formal sector termed "urban work force" clearly defined in the organizational or legal sense, such a sector can be conceived of as the people residing in urban areas, having higher educational levels, and employed in either industrial or tertiary (service) occupations. It is the degree of integration of Ukrainians into the advanced work force of the Ukrainian SSR, particularly in comparison with Russians, that provides the focus of this study. The urban work force is viewed as representative of advanced Soviet society, advanced relative to rural areas in socioeconomic levels. No attempt is made here to assess changes in or different

levels of advancement by nationalities within the advanced urban
work force; data reflecting on this question are scarce and often of
questionable relevance, being confined to very small segments of
society such as the Ukrainian Academy of Sciences.

Two sources of data were used to measure the integration of
Ukrainians into the advanced work force, and their interaction with
other ethnic groups: (1) data from the 1959 and 1970 Soviet Censuses,[1]
and (2) a review of the major Ukrainian-language newspaper of the
Ukrainian SSR, Radians'ka Ukraina, for the period August 1, 1972
through January 21, 1973, for articles indicating the participation of
ethnic groups in the advanced work force.

In order to utilize census data for the study of the integration
of Ukrainians and others into the advanced work force of the Ukrainian
SSR, it was necessary to define operationally variables characteristic
of participation in this sector. The variables selected as representative of modernization and integration into the advanced sector of
society were:

(1) Level of Urbanization by Unit: defined as the number of
persons residing in urban centers (census definition) as a percentage
of the total population of each oblast. Urbanization in the Soviet context subsumes many indicators of modernization, since virtually all
industry and the majority of advanced employment is located in the
cities, and educational levels are significantly higher in urban areas
than in rural areas. For instance, in the Ukrainian SSR in 1970, 72
percent of blue collar workers (rabochie) and 82 percent of white
collar workers (sluzhashchie) were classified as urban, and the urban
population had roughly twice the level of educational attainment of
the rural population.[2]

(2) Level of Education by Unit: defined as the percentage of the
total population of each oblast having higher or secondary education
(including incomplete secondary).

(3) Advanced Work Force by Unit: defined as the percentage of
the total population of each oblast classified as blue collar and white
collar workers, and their dependents.

(4) Percentage of Urban Population by ethnic group: the percentage of the urban population in each oblast comprised by each
ethnic group.

These variables were then spatially correlated with ethnic composition as the dependent variable for the twenty-five oblasts of the
Ukrainian SSR. It should be noted that correlations of two or more
variables across a number of spatially-ordered units provide a measure of the association of phenomena in space, and are a convenient
way of summarizing the associations between phenomena. In a strict

sense, cause-effect relationships can only be inferred from measures of association. Therefore, data for the entire Republic, cross-tabulated by nationality, will be utilized to substantiate the associational relationships.

Evidence of nationality integration and interaction in the advanced work force was also sought in the local press. The following criteria were employed to select information indicative of such interaction: (1) direct statements, such as editorials or decrees, about the necessity or desirability of participation by nationalities in the advanced work force, and (2) news articles in which nationalities are named in conjunction with some aspect of the advanced work force.

The Ukrainian SSR is second among the 15 Union Republics of the Soviet Union in population (after the RSFSR) and third in area (after the RSFSR and Kazakhstan). In 1970 it had roughly four times the population of the third most populous republic, Kazakhstan.[3] With approximately three percent of the area and 20 percent of the population of the Soviet Union, the Ukraine produces 31 percent of the country's natural gas, 33 percent of the coal, 57 percent of the iron ore, and 40 percent of the steel.[4]

The Ukraine is divided administratively into twenty-five oblasts of approximately equal area and population, with the exception of Donetsk Oblast, which alone accounts for over ten percent of the Republic's population. The heavy industrial capacity responsible for the majority of production in the Ukraine is clustered in several oblasts. Heavy industry and mining are concentrated in the Eastern Ukraine around the Donets coal basin, in an area including Voroshilovgrad and Donetsk Oblasts, around the bend of the Dnepr in Dnepropetrovsk and Zaporozh'e Oblasts, and around the iron ore deposits at Krivoi Rog and the manganese deposits at Nikopol'. Major natural gas producing areas are located near Shebelinka in Khar'kov Oblast and Dashava in L'vov Oblast. Khar'kov is a major center of diversified manufacturing.[5]

The location of these regions of heavy and extractive industry is important for this inquiry, because the advanced urban work force naturally will be concentrated in these areas. For example, in 1959 five oblasts (Voroshilovgrad, Donetsk, Dnepropetrovsk, Zaporozh'e and Khar'kov) with 32 percent of the total population of the Ukraine, accounted for 48 percent of blue collar workers and 37 percent of white collar workers in the Republic.[6]

By examining the distributions of ethnic groups in the Ukraine, and relating these distributions to concentrations of urban-industrial centers, the geographic basis can be found for examining the integration of groups into modernized sectors of society. The Ukrainians are distributed very evenly among all oblasts and areas of the Ukraine, with no single oblast having a disproportionate number of Ukrainians relative to the distribution of the total population. Approximately equal numbers of Ukrainians are found in predominantly rural, agricultural areas and in urban, industrial areas. The Russians, on the other hand, are highly concentrated in areas of industry and urbanization. In 1970, 76 percent of all Russians in the Ukraine were located in seven of the 25 oblasts: Voroshilovgrad, Donetsk, Crimea, Zaporozh'e, Khar'kov, Odessa, and Dnepropetrovsk.[7]

The ethnic composition of the urban-industrial areas of the Ukraine is naturally a reflection of these distributions. Although Ukrainians comprise a majority of the population in these areas, their share of that population is significantly lower than their share of the total Republic population. Contrariwise, the Russians comprise a disproportionately large share of the population in the urban-industrial areas relative to their share of the total Republic population. In 1970, the Russians comprised 33.2 percent of the population of the five major industrial oblasts (Voroshilovgrad, Donetsk, Zaporozh'e, Khar'kov and Dnepropetrovsk) and 19.4 percent of the population of the Republic. The Ukrainians accounted for 61.8 percent of the population of these units, and 74.9 percent of the total population of the Ukraine in 1970.[8]

The results of the statistical analysis of socioeconomic variables representing modernization and their relationships to the geographic distribution of ethnic groups revealed the expected patterns. From the bivariate correlation coefficients for ethnic composition (the dependent variable) and the indicators of the advanced urban-industrial work force (independent variables) as presented in Table 1, it is quite clear that on this geographic scale the Russians are highly associated and the Ukrainians highly negatively associated with modernization. The consistent relationships are evident because the indicators of modernization are closely related to one another—areas of high urbanization are also areas of higher educational levels and larger proportions of workers in industry and tertiary sectors.

These statistical relationships show that, on the oblast scale, the higher the levels of urbanization, education, and advanced work force, the higher is the percentage of Russians in the oblast population. On the other hand, the higher the levels of modernization as measured by selected indices, the lower is the percentage of Ukrainians in the population. These relationships do not come as a surprise, inasmuch as traditional Ukrainian areas characterized by rural, agricultural populations, influence the spatial association of Ukrainians with the indicators of modernization. Ukrainians are distributed evenly throughout the Republic, and millions of Ukrainians live in the industrial areas of the Eastern Ukraine (in fact, they constitute a majority in that region). How can it be then, that these correlations do not take into account the significant numbers of Ukrainians in these urban-industrial areas? The answer is that the vast majority of

TABLE 1

Rank Order (Spearman) Correlation Coefficients
(Bivariate) for Stated Indices, Ukrainians
and Russians in 25 Oblasts of Ukrainian
SSR, 1959 and 1970
(in percentages)

Ethnic group	Urban	1959 Ad.WF	Ed.
Ukrainians	-.815	-.817	-.704
Russians	.919	.879	.858
		1970	
Ukrainians	-.780	-.780	-.719
Russians	.921	.822	.820

Sources: 1959 data from: Itogi vsesoiuznoi perepisi naseleniia 1959 goda, Ukrainskaia SSR (Moscow: Gosstatizdat, 1963). 1970 data from: Itogi vsesoiuznoi perepisi naseleniia 1970 goda (Moscow: Statistika, 1972-73), I-V.

Ukrainians in the Ukraine live in the more traditional agricultural areas, and therefore the urban Ukrainians are in effect submerged in the total, at least on this scale of analysis.

Using correlations between variables ordered into units as large as oblasts introduces another bias, the fallacy of assuming that within a given unit all Russians are characterized by high levels of integration into the advanced sectors or, on the other hand, Ukrainians are all kolkhozniki (collective farm workers). Aggregate data available for the Republic as a whole on the extent of modernization by ethnic group shed additional light on the degree to which each group has been integrated into advanced sectors. In 1970, Ukrainians in the Ukraine were 46 percent urban, whereas Russians in the Ukraine were 85 percent urban.[9] In 1970, the educational levels for Ukrainians in the Republic were lower than the levels for the Russians. Of the total population of Ukrainians, 46 percent had attained higher or secondary education (including incomplete secondary), whereas the comparable figure for the Russians was 61 percent. In urban areas the difference between educational levels for Ukrainians and Russians was very small, 61 and 64 percent respectively.[10] This again illustrates that when the total population is considered, the large rural Ukrainian component has the effect of lowering the level of modernization of

Ukrainians in the Ukraine, because rural levels of education and advanced employment are naturally much lower than in urban areas.

Very little data reflecting directly on the integration of ethnic groups into the advanced work force of the Ukraine are available. One Soviet source showed that Russians provided a disproportionately large share of specialists with higher and specialized education (engineers, agronomists, and the like), and Ukrainians a disproportionately small share.[11] The same relative disproportions have been noted elsewhere. One Soviet Ukrainian dissident reported data indicating that the Ukrainian share of scientists and scholars in the Ukraine in 1960 was 48.3 percent, whereas Ukrainians comprised 76.8 percent of the Republic's population.[12]

In 1970, Jews ranked third in size among ethnic groups in the Ukraine, and Belorussians ranked fourth.[13] Data on educational and urbanization levels for these two nationalities suggest that their role in the social and economic spheres of the Ukraine complements that of the Russians—highly modernized outsiders (many of the Jews, of course, are not outsiders in the strict sense of the word). In 1959, Jews and Belorussians ranked first and second respectively in levels of educational attainment for the Ukrainian SSR, ahead of the Russians and considerably ahead of the indigenous Ukrainians.[14] The Jews were more urbanized than Russians or Ukrainians, and the Belorussians were significantly more urbanized than Ukrainians and almost equal to the level of the Russians.[15] Although these two nationalities are highly modernized, their small size relative to Ukrainians and Russians in the Republic somewhat reduces their impact on advanced sectors of society. In 1970, Jews accounted for only 1.6 percent and Belorussians .8 percent of the population of the Ukrainian SSR.[16]

Therefore, it can be inferred from these statistical relationships and aggregate data that Ukrainians in their own Republic do not participate in advanced sectors of society to the degree warranted by their numbers. The majority of Ukrainians remain rural dwellers, whereas other ethnic groups, particularly Russians, occupy large shares of the urban-industrial sectors. One reason for the underrepresentation of Ukrainians in these areas possibly involves Soviet policy designed to shift young skilled personnel from their titular republic to other areas.[17] Also, research in the social sciences points to considerable voluntary migration in many societies by young persons in response to economic opportunities.[18] A combination of these two forces might account for the higher levels of modernization among Ukrainians residing outside of their own Republic. On the average, Ukrainians outside the Ukraine achieve higher levels of education, urbanization, and skilled employment than do those in the Ukraine.[19] This point is relevant if large numbers of young, skilled Ukrainian workers are assigned or move to areas outside the Ukraine, and Russians and others move in to take job opportunities in the UkSSR. Thus, it is possible that many potential Ukrainian entrants into the advanced urban-industrial sectors are siphoned off, leaving mainly rural Ukrainians.

In the six months of the daily Ukrainian-language newspaper Radians'ka Ukraina reviewed for articles reflecting the interaction and integration of nationalities in the advanced work force, the evidence was surprisingly meager. Over 150 issues of the newspaper were surveyed, yet only four articles were discovered which met the criteria described earlier (specific mention of nationalities in the advanced work force or editorials and decrees advocating nationality cooperation in the work force). Two articles described the multinational composition of groups of industrial workers; in one instance, a group constructing a petroleum pipeline in Zakarpatsk Oblast, in the other instance, the work force of a shipyard in Nikolaev.[20] Two other articles, one a decree from Party First Secretary Brezhnev and the other a TASS editorial, reminded readers of the necessity for working together with other nationalities in the development of the economy and culture.[21] In no instance were nationalities, not even Ukrainians, specifically named as participants in the advanced work force.

Considering the size and multinational character of the work force in the Ukraine, the lack of space devoted to such an important topic seems odd. Possibly, articles of the type sought in this study appear in profusion in more specialized publications, such as trade union journals. Yet, the message carried to the general populace is of major importance, and for six months this message virtually ignored the multinational character of the work force in the Ukraine. Although other possibilities exist that would qualify this interpretation, such as the ability of the readership to associate individuals' names with nationality or the random element in reporting, it seems likely that the interaction and integration of nationalities in the advanced work force is not a major theme of the principal Ukrainian-language newspaper.

Any assessment of the lack of press coverage given to the multinational character of the work force is, of course, speculative. Criticism against inroads into the advanced sectors of the Ukraine by outsiders is a point raised by the dissident intellectual Ivan Dzyuba, and such incursions may be a source of alienation among educated Ukrainians.[22] If faced with discontent among Ukrainians on this point, the Soviet government could react in two ways through its control of the media: (1) barrage the populace with articles illustrating the multinational character of the advanced sector in the Ukraine and the benefits allegedly accruing therefrom, or (2) ignore the topic altogether. The press coverage analyzed for this study suggests the application of the latter policy.

In conclusion, although there are millions of Ukrainians who have been integrated into advanced Soviet society via the process of modernization (urbanization, education, industrialization), the Ukrainians in the Ukraine remain characterized by lower levels of modernization and integration into the advanced work force than the Russians and the nationalities in the Republic. Large numbers of Russians continue to migrate to the Ukraine, as evidenced by the large increase (28.7 percent) in Russians in the Ukraine between 1959 and 1970. Available evidence suggests that these Russians move mainly to industrial areas.

It has already been noted that the Ukrainians outside of the Ukraine are more modernized than those within their own Republic. The case can be made that this also applies to Russians (and to Belorussians and others); namely, that Russians in the Ukraine are more modernized than those in traditional Russians areas of the RSFSR. It might seem logical, therefore, to insist on a comparison of the Russians in the Ukraine with the Ukrainians in the RSFSR before reaching any conclusion about relative levels of modernization. Yet it is the ethnic basis of the Soviet federation which lends importance to the levels of modernization of nationalities within their titular republics. The point is, therefore, not only that Ukrainians in Kazakhstan are more highly modernized than Kazakhs or Ukrainians in the Ukraine, but that many of these Ukrainians have left their own Republic, for whatever reasons.

The relative size discrepancies between the Russians and the nationalities renders this exchange of population more "visible" for the non-Russian areas. For example, in 1970 there were 9,126,000 Russians in the Ukraine, amounting to 19.4 percent of the Republic's population. Also in 1970, there were 3,346,000 Ukrainians in the RSFSR, yet they accounted for only 2.6 percent of the population of the RSFSR. The relatively small size of the Ukraine (and other republics) in comparison with the RSFSR means that an equal exchange of population between the RSFSR and any republic will result in the Russians being much more prominent in the non-Russian areas.

If Soviet policy does in fact advocate the incorporation of Ukrainians into modernized society, some assessment of the success of such a policy and its implications must be attempted. Soviet policy generally seems to encourage the integration of nationalities into the modern economy, if for no other reason than to meet labor requirements.[23] Indeed, the leveling of society so that all nationalities may reach roughly equal socioeconomic status may be a moral or humanitarian policy on the part of the Soviet government. Indications are that at the very least, the removal of economic and social barriers to the integration of groups into modern society is viewed as a prerequisite for the creation of a truly Soviet people. Yet, there is evidence which implies that this integration often means the assignment of skilled personnel to areas outside their nationality areas.[24]

Aside from policies directly influencing the integration of nationalities into the industrial and tertiary work force, other policies exert an indirect effect on the redistribution of nationalities. Economic development and industrial location policies are obvious examples. The expansion of industry in a given area probably creates job opportunities in excess of the numbers and skills of the indigenous population, necessitating the in-migration of workers (many of whom may be outsiders). This demand is further heightened if skilled indigenous personnel are being assigned or voluntarily leaving for jobs outside of their nationality area. In the case of the Ukrainian SSR, it would appear that both direct and indirect effects of policies are resulting in the in-migration of Russians and others into the urban-industrial areas of the Republic.

Thus, it is the relative position of one group vis-à-vis another which is held to be of importance. The perception of relative disadvantage is, after all, the critical point in the final analysis. Some limited evidence suggests that Ukrainian dissidents do indeed perceive the incursions by Russians into the advanced sectors of society in the Ukraine. Of far greater importance is whether or not the general populace, particularly those in the lower socioeconomic strata, perceives the Russians and other outsiders as usurpers of opportunities within the Ukraine. Feelings over this relative disadvantage may be exacerbated by the ethnic basis of the Soviet federation, for Ukrainians may consider certain advantages due them in their own republic. Within the advanced work force sector of society, a sector characteristic of modern Soviet society (urban, industrial, educated), the Ukrainians remain less modernized than the Russians and other main nationalities of the Republic. Ethnic tensions and the individuality of Ukrainians will persist at least until the time they reach socioeconomic parity with the Russians in the Ukraine.

The importance of the integration of the other nationalities of the Soviet West into advanced sectors of society within their titular republics is basically the same as for the situation in the Ukraine. The Estonians and Latvians are more modernized than the other groups, but the Russians are gaining ground in advanced sectors in these republics because low levels of indigenous workers are entering the labor force, low levels resulting from very low rates of population growth among these two nationalities. As in the Ukrainian experience, the other three republics, Lithuania, Belorussia, and Moldavia, can expect large in-migrations of Russians and others as economic development continues in these relatively underdeveloped areas. The Ukraine assumes added importance because of its geographic size and location and its large population, but the processes of modernization and integration of indigenous nationalities are of great significance to the nationality question in the Soviet West and to the maintenance of the Soviet ethnic federation.

NOTES

1. 1959 data are from Itogi vsesoiuznoi perepisi naseleniia 1959 goda, Ukrainskaia SSR (Moscow: Gosstatizdat, 1963). 1970 data are from Itogi vsesoiuznoi perepisi naseleniia 1970 goda (Moscow: Statistika, 1972-73), I-V. These two sources are hereafter abbreviated as Itogi 1959 and Itogi 1970, respectively.

2. Itogi 1970, IV, pp. 32-33, 56-57; V, p. 8.

3. Narodnoe khoziaistvo SSSR v 1970 g. (Moscow: Statistika, 1971), p. 12.

4. Ibid., p. 70.

5. Theodore Shabad, Basic Industrial Resources of the U.S.S.R. (New York: Columbia University Press, 1969), pp. 173-99.

6. Itogi 1959, pp. 70-71.

7. Itogi 1970, IV, pp. 152-91.

8. Ibid.

9. Ibid., pp. 152-63.

10. Ibid., pp. 475-76.

11. Reported in Yaroslav Bilinsky, "Assimilation and Ethnic Assertiveness Among Ukrainians of the Soviet Union," in Ethnic Minorities in the Soviet Union, ed. Erich Goldhagen (New York: Praeger, 1968), p. 152.

12. Ivan Dzyuba, Internationalism or Russification? 2nd ed. (London: Weidenfeld and Nicolson, 1970), pp. 122-123.

13. Itogi 1970, IV, pp. 152-53.

14. Itogi 1959, pp. 194-95.

15. Ibid., pp. 168-70.

16. Itogi 1970, pp. 152-53.

17. Bilinsky, pp. 153-156.

18. C. J. Jansen, "Migration: A Sociological Problem," in Readings in the Sociology of Migration, ed. Clifford J. Jansen (Oxford: Pergamon, 1970), p. 14.

19. Data on the levels of urbanization of Ukrainians outside the Ukraine can be figured by using Union-wide and Ukrainian SSR volumes for 1959. In 1959, Ukrainians residing outside the Ukraine were 55.2 percent urban. See Itogi vsesoiuznoi perepisi naseleniia 1959 goda, SSSR (Moscow: Gosstatizdat, 1962), pp. 184, 190. Data on the levels of education for Ukrainians outside the Ukraine are in Itogi . . . Ukrainskaia SSR, p. 194. In 1959, 35.2 percent of those Ukrainians

outside the Ukraine had attained higher or secondary education (including incomplete secondary), whereas the comparable figure for those in the Ukraine was 27.8 percent.

20. "Simvol ednannia," Radians'ka Ukraina, November 26, 1972, p. 3.

21. "Za druzhbu i spivrobitnitsvo," Radians'ka Ukraina, October 7, 1972, p. 1. "Uchasnikam mizhnarodnoi naukovoi konferentsii v Tashkenti," Radians'ka Ukraina, October 17, 1972, p. 1.

22. Dzyuba, pp. 122-23.

23. See A. I. Kholmogorov, Internationsional'ne cherty sovetskikh natsii (Moscow: Mysl', 1970).

24. Bilinsky, pp. 151-56.

6

SOVIET EFFORTS AT THE SOCIOECONOMIC INTEGRATION OF LATVIANS

Mary Ann Grossman

On December 20, 1972, the Union of Soviet Socialist Republics celebrated the fiftieth anniversary of its federation as an entity which is "nationalist in form and socialist in content." The 15 constituent republics of the federation marked their jubilee year in numerous ways which ranged from a heightened interest in the activities of "Brother Republics" to the early fulfillment of the year's production quotas. Despite the many successes achieved by the Soviet federation within the past 50 years, the processes of political, economic, social, and cultural integration continue. In fact, the fiftieth anniversary celebration may be viewed as a renewed effort to spur the process of integrating the diverse nationality groups that comprise the Soviet Union.

Within the Latvian Republic, groups such as the Komsomol, and to a lesser extent, the labor unions and the Latvian Communist party, exert pressure for the integration and mobilization of society within the Soviet West; pressure which is intended to diminish the vitality of the Latvian nationality. Although they are obliged to interact with these groups which work for integration, Latvians in general tend to maintain a traditional and well-defined nationality profile that is supported by a predilection for non-interaction with other ethnic groups.

To provide a means of measuring the effectiveness of these pressures for integration, an analysis of specific group interactions within the socioeconomic sector of Latvian society will be conducted. It is evident from the current press consulted for this study that both integrative and divisive forces are active within the Republic. The major research resources were two daily Russian-language news-papers published within the Latvian SSR, Sovetskaia Latviia (surveyed for September 1972 through February 1973), and Sovetskaia molodezh', the Republic's Komsomol paper (surveyed from November 1972 to February 1973).

Within the Latvian SSR, various economic and social groups provide a framework for the interaction of integrative and divisive forces. Integration and divisiveness, for the purposes of this paper, will be examined as two opposing processes that occur within this socioeconomic sphere. The term integration is restricted to mean the dedication of economic and social efforts to a larger "Soviet society." Thus, integration tends to diminish specific Latvian nationality pride (or nationality divisiveness) by subordinating it to goals of cooperation with other republics of the Soviet West and to the development of the total Soviet society. Integration is not to be confused here with the concept "Russification" which denotes cultural and perhaps linguistic assimilation. Rather, integration will be analyzed here within the bounds of Latvia's economic and social spheres as an attempt to establish economic and social coordination and cooperation between the Latvian SSR and its neighboring republics in the Soviet West.

Conversely, the term divisiveness denotes those attitudes and actions on the part of certain groups that tend to enhance the enduring traits of Latvian nationality, the foremost of these traits being pride in national accomplishments. Thus, those groups characterized by divisive sympathies emphasize social and economic goals for the development of the Latvian Republic and its titular nationality. In their reluctance to subordinate developmental goals to the larger Soviet society, these proponents of divisiveness stand in direct opposition to those groups advocating Latvian integration.

These opposing forces have been directed upon, among others, a particular segment of Latvian society—the youthful workers of Latvian industry and agriculture. The Republic's highly developed and continually modernizing industrial sector is given great emphasis in the local press. In this way, Latvian industry emerges simultaneously as a prime component of the Latvian nationality profile within the Republic and as a fruitful area in which to investigate the integrative forces acting upon that nationality profile.

It has been necessary to extend this research beyond the sphere of industry and the enterprise as such to examine the accompanying social aspects of industrial production. In filling the ranks of labor, exclusive of in-migration, the greatest single labor reserve is the Latvian youth enrolled in secondary educational institutions. The comprehensive educational process (vospitanie) of potential socialist laborers thus becomes a vital area for integration, and will be examined in some detail below.

Within the ambit of this socioeconomic sector, several groups comprise the two opposing forces of integration and divisiveness which contend for the loyalty of Latvian youth. Forces for Latvian integration with other republics of the Soviet West consist primarily of the

Komsomol organizations within the factory and the school, for these Komsomol cells provide frequent and direct contact with youth. Less directly, the unions which sponsor "socialist competition" in labor, and the Latvian Communist party, also work for the integration of Latvian youth into the larger society. Integrative terms are used most frequently by these groups. The processes of education and economic production then, are subsumed under the greater goals of "brotherhood of nations" and "socialist construction."

The group that seemingly reinforces Latvian nationality consciousness is comprised of managers of enterprises and of collective and state farms. Instructors in secondary schools and Latvian educators also exhort youth to study diligently in preparation for their entry into Latvian industry. Their exhortations provide the most direct link between education and the enterprise. Young people are advised to choose a vocational field of study carefully, and articles and advertisements appear frequently that inform students enrolled in a particular vocational institution of specific jobs available in related enterprises. It is most significant that no "integrative terms" such as "socialist competition," "social debt," or "brotherhood of labor" appear in these articles. These opposing integrative and divisive forces will be examined in greater detail below, and will be analyzed for a measure of their effectiveness.

In conjunction with the interdisciplinary method adopted by the entire seminar group, interaction will be examined and assessed on two levels. The first level of analysis concerns the Latvian Republic. On the second level, these findings will be related to interactions between Latvia and its neighboring republics within the Soviet West. In this way, the question of nationality may be viewed with specific reference to the Latvian nationality and subsequently may be extended to the Soviet West as a whole.

In utilizing Latvia as a focal point, the developments surrounding the Latvian nationality question may be viewed as important components of the larger issue within the Soviet West. The nature and scope of interactions both within the Latvian SSR and between it and other republics of the Soviet West can further illuminate the complex question of nationality in the Soviet West today. Identifying specific types of interactions between groups and measuring the intensity of these interactions will provide a description of the present situation within the Republic and a projection of trends which may continue in the immediate future for both the Latvian Republic and the Soviet West.

The phrase "the Latvian predilection for non-interaction" with other nationality units has great significance for both recent history and the present situation. Latvian aloofness from other republics of the Soviet West bears upon the ability of Latvians to resist the current

Soviet efforts for integration. The development of Latvian industry during the independence period (1918-1940) and the Soviet period (1940 onward) appears to have been a prime sustaining factor for Latvia's indifference to interaction with neighboring republics.

Historically, the German and Swedish occupations of Latvia and Estonia left a distinctive political and cultural imprint upon the two republics, an imprint that has facilitated their modernization process.[1] Geographically, the location of the three Baltic states, Latvia, Estonia, and Lithuania has given them the status of "transmission belts" for the flow of Western ideas into the Russian Empire and, later, into the Soviet Union.[2] It has been argued that the vast extent of Baltic contacts with the West is reflected in the present economic development of the republics, for in each republic emphasis is placed upon light industry, which demands highly skilled labor and few raw materials.[3]

Despite the fact that the different nationalities were subject to these similar currents of political and economic development, Baltic cohesion was never strong enough to promote a lasting Baltic federation. During the independence period the political situation provided the greatest opportunity for some form of Baltic federation; however, this political goal was never effectively pursued. A strong ethnocentric tendency within each country supplied the prime deterrent to federation; each nationality believed that the sovereign nation-state offered the best means of preserving strong ethnic identity.[4]

Language differences have also worked against federation. Despite their geographical proximity, Latvians and Estonians cannot converse without the aid of interpreters. Linguistically, the Estonians maintain strong connections with Finnish and related languages, and culturally, the Lithuanians have absorbed much that is Polish in origin. In this way, cultural and linguistic ties between Latvia and her sister Baltic republics remained minimal. This history of Latvian cultural and linguistic separateness has carried over to the contemporary situation, for despite a movement toward economic integration, references to cultural and linguistic collaboration with other republics are notably few in the local press.

Industrial development has advanced rapidly in all the Baltic republics since World War II. Much of Baltic industry had been destroyed by the war, and most of its labor force was dispersed. By the end of the war, the number of industrial workers in Latvia had fallen to 65 percent of what it had been in 1940 (the comparable figure for the Soviet Union as a whole during this period was 85 percent). The numerical growth of the Baltic working class from this low point was extremely rapid. By 1950, the number of workers in Latvia had increased to 149 percent of the 1940 level.[5]

This remarkable increase in the labor force has remained a source of pride for the Latvians to the present day. Because the Baltic area, and Latvia in particular, does not produce major industrial raw materials of importance to the economy of the Soviet Union, its industrial development has moved chiefly along the line of manufacturing products which require relatively small amounts of raw materials, but are of high value.[6] However, highly skilled and educated workers are required for the more complex tasks of the major industries in electronics and radio engineering, precision instrument making, chemical and glass fiber development, computer technology, and food processing.[7]

Inevitably linked with its advanced local economy, Latvia has attained an educational level for its population higher than the Soviet average. In 1970, 51.7 percent of the Latvian SSR population had received at least some high school education; in the entire USSR, the corresponding figure was 48.3 percent.[8]

Command of a skilled labor force has enabled the Latvian Republic to maintain one of the highest standards of living in the Soviet Union. According to estimates prepared by Western economists, the per capita income for Latvians in 1969 was 1,515 rubles ($1,680), as compared with 1,071 rubles ($1,188) for the Soviet Union as a whole.[9] This higher standard of living enjoyed by the Latvians has attracted increasing numbers of Russians from neighboring areas to settle in Riga and other urban industrial centers. Within the 11 years following 1959, the number of people moving to Latvia—158,000—has far exceeded the 114,000 added to the population by natural increase.[10]

With the influx of Russian workers, the Latvian share of the 2.4 million population in the Republic has decreased in recent years. In 1969, the birthrate in Latvia was 14 births per thousand population, the lowest for any republic in the Soviet Union. Conversely, the death rate, at 11.1 per thousand, ranks second highest Union-wide, after that of Estonia. Thus, the rate of natural increase of the population of Latvia in 1969 (birth rate minus death rate) was only 2.9 per thousand, the least increase of any republic. In comparison, the natural increase rate for the Soviet Union as a whole during this year was 8.9 per thousand.[11]

The growing proportion of the Russian labor force in the Republic causes deep concern to older Latvians. This generation fears that the Latvian nationality and its cultural heritage will soon be absorbed by a Russian-dominated Soviet society. Youthful Latvians appear to have less political consciousness, for their primary concerns are economic.[12] Thus, the older generation of Latvians considers it imperative to increase the nationality consciousness of Latvian youth, for these young people will have to compete with Russian laborers for positions within Latvian industry. In this way, the proponents of nationality consciousness hope to preserve the unique nature of Latvian industrial enterprise from Soviet encroachment.

In 1971, Latvian factory managers opposed plans for erecting large-scale industrial and power plants on the grounds that such projects would alter the form of Latvian industry and thus stimulate great in-migrations of non-Latvian workers. In a speech to the Latvian Communist Party Congress, Secretary A. E. Voss severely criticized such "national narrowmindedness." "They do not understand," he said, "that Communist construction cannot be achieved without the tightest political, economic and cultural cooperation, and without the mutual assistance of all peoples of the USSR."[13]

By 1972, despite these initial protests, new industrial sites were developed in Latvia along with an influx of non-Latvian workers. In a letter of protest sent to foreign Communist parties, seventeen Latvian Communists complained that the Republic has

> a number of large enterprises where there are almost no Latvians among the workers, engineering, technical personnel and directors . . . in all republic, city and district organizations, in most local organizations and in all enterprises, business is conducted in Russian.[14]

Given their great vested interest in retaining control of Latvia's highly complex industrial enterprises, and in the educational qualifications of a Latvian labor force, it follows that both local managers of enterprises and educators regard vocational education as a critical formative factor bearing directly upon the question of nationality consciousness. In this regard, achieving a high standard of educational quality becomes a prerequisite for the technological and scientific advances to be made in industry. Forces for Latvian nationality consciousness, industrial managers and educators have repeatedly emphasized these goals in the Republic's press. As a counter-force to this nationality divisiveness, partisans of integration have made higher standards in education and industry synonymous with cooperation among nationalities and the construction of socialism.

THE ROLE AND IMPORTANCE OF INDUSTRY IN LATVIA

Industrial production, according to Soviet definition, includes urban enterprise and the state and collective farms. This is the foremost area of activity covered by Sovetskaia Latviia. Latvian industry, with its achievements and needs, is meticulously examined—and extolled—as a self-contained unit. Specific references are rarely if ever made concerning industrial trade or cooperation with other republics of the Soviet West; however, more general references to the importance of the "Communist laborer" or to the "cooperation of nationalities" appear in these writings, although infrequently.

Throughout Sovetskaia Latviia, short informative articles often describe the achievements of Latvian industry. These brief articles are laudatory, in contrast to longer, more thoughtful articles that expound industry's problems. For example, in November 1972 a report heralded the release of the first solid-state, stereophonic radio-phonograph to be produced in the USSR. The Latvian radio plant named in honor of A. S. Potov issued the first experimental models of a new "radio-grammophone," the "Victoria," and exhibited these models in Czechoslovakia, the German Democratic Republic, Austria, and the United States.[15] In January 1973, this same enterprise released 10,000 units of this model for domestic and foreign markets.[16]

A measure of Latvian pride in its industrial sector is provided here, for the publicity specifically noted that this Latvian enterprise provided the first transistorized phonograph in the USSR and that these models were exhibited abroad. A second important implication of these reports is that Latvia is at the scientific and technological forefront of industry within the Soviet Union.

The Republic's amalgamated "Latsel'khoztekhnika" (Latvian Agricultural Technology) was formed in 1970 in order to direct the "growth of the volume of production and the widening of industrial output . . . [by means of] a system of economic and mathematical methods, electronic calculation and other contemporary technology."[17] This use of data processing for agricultural planning is characteristic of the advanced state of the Latvian economy. The yearly output of goods, Latvia's material base, has grown to 55 million rubles. Latsel'khoztekhnika developed a computer center in 1970 to deal with the problems of nomenclature and distribution in commodity circulation. This new system has achieved positive results, for problems are quickly solved according to the calculations of the movement of goods. According to reports, the material-technical provision of the kolkhozy and sovkhozy has been adequately met through the center's operation.[18]

These facts illustrate the Latvian initiative in directing the output and flow of its industrial goods. More important, the Republic's economy has developed to a high technological level which makes data processing a reality. Through the sophisticated products of its industry, the Latvian SSR can better plan and maintain that same productive process.

Latvian pride in industrial achievement is tacitly expressed in reports that describe the efforts of local industry to serve local needs. One such report outlines the work of a plant in the town of Kengarags producing reinforced concrete sections. A new school designed to serve 1,712 pupils will be constructed from prefabricated, reinforced sections supplied by the local plants. Upon completion, it will be the largest secondary school in the Latvian SSR.[19]

These accounts should be distinguished from those which cite the achievements of Latvian industry within the context of the Five-Year Plan. During October 1972, numerous references were made to the early fulfillment of the productive plan within various industries. Usually these achievements were said to be accomplished in commemoration of the fiftieth anniversary of the Soviet federation. Thus, in these articles, the national pride and sense of accomplishment is subordinated to integrative efforts. In announcing the exceeding of its production quota for ventilators and air-valves during the second year of the current Five-Year Plan (1972), the personnel of a plant in Ventspils provided such an example: "Not one of the large projects stipulated in the Five-Year Plan could have been completed without the plant's [contribution of] component parts. [Moreover], our product is in popular demand, not only within the country but also abroad; it is readily purchased in thirty countries of the world."[20]

The statement continues in praise of the great accomplishments achieved in 50 years of political and economic federation, and more specifically, to praise the efforts of the Communist laborer. The author holds the significant title of Secretary of the Party Bureau in the plant. The staff had decided to surpass the initial planned goal of completing 5,500 air-valves in honor of the jubilee year commemorating the Soviet federation. Yet these successes were attributed solely to the factory Party organization composed of seventy CPSU members.[21]

In this way, the Party cell within the factory emerges as the entity exerting the most frequent and sustained effort for the integration of the Latvian workers into the larger Soviet economy. The labor union also provides a means of integration, most notably through programs of "socialist competition" in production. However, when the Party acts in collaboration with the labor unions, more tangible goals are proposed which can be achieved through concrete means—the heightening of productive output through the competition of various enterprises within the republics of the Soviet West. Thus, in the Riga Diesel Construction Plant, which has captured many first-prize banners in socialist competition, the workers' high production is attributed to "socialist competition . . . [in which] one hundred workers of the plant worked out personal plans for increasing output, including in the competition the meeting of quotas for the Five-Year Plan ahead of time."[22]

In the above instance, socialist competition is said also to encompass socialist collaboration. A reference to the cooperative production efforts of several Union republics—the single reference to interrepublic cooperation to be found in Sovetskaia Latviia during the six-month period under investigation—emphasizes that the contributions of other regions had made successes possible. The spokesman, once again a secretary of a factory Party committee, praised the socialist republics of the Ukraine, Armenia, Azerbaijan, and Russia for delivering their supplies of construction tools and parts. Although these republics represent a diversity of regions within the Soviet Union and not the Soviet West in particular, cooperative effort on an interrepublic level is clearly stated.[23]

INTEGRATIVE AND DIVISIVE FORCES IN EDUCATION

Divisive and integrative efforts are consistently focused upon Latvian youth. Acquiring technical expertise and a complete general eduational background for future workers is encouraged by divisive and integrative groups alike. The compulsory eight-year school, the present standard of universal secondary education in the Soviet Union, constitutes a primary center upon which efforts for both divisiveness and integration are directed.

The educational process undergone by the laborer takes him through the eight-year school and additional study for two-to-three years in a specialized secondary school, or within the factory itself. Educators and industrial managers of the Latvian SSR are extremely conscious of the need for more highly qualified workers to meet new scientific and technological demands of further industrialization. The Komsomol, as well, is aware of this need. Thus, these two opposing forces compete for the custody of the youthful laborer.

The student who becomes a dropout (otsev) from the secondary school appears to cause great concern to Latvian educators. Although no figures for a dropout rate are revealed, there are attempts to deal with the problem. An instructor in a workers' school in Riga (a "shift" school) which enables young workers to continue their education writes that the most difficult problem facing schools for working youth is the retention of the entire student body for the length of the school year. He suggests that the reason students drop out is because there are weak connections between pedagogy and the enterprises in which the young people work while they attend classes. In this instance, it is felt, the teacher must supersede the Party organization.[24] The educator, recognizing that the Party, labor union, and Komsomol support universal secondary education, still maintains that reaching educational goals is primarily the responsibility of the teacher. Furthermore, the problem of dropouts is specifically addressed to schools for working youth. Thus, a close connection between the Latvian educational system and Latvian labor is maintained.

Becoming a member of the Latvian working class is synonymous with some type of vocational education (called professional-technical education throughout the Soviet Union.) The biography of a young peasant girl who joins a factory built in Daugavpils during the first years of the Soviet federation reveals that she received vocational training under the auspices of the chemical fiber plant. Upon completion of the course, she acquired a specialty in weaving and an assistant master rating in spinning.[25] No reference is made to the Komsomol organization or the trade union in the process of this young woman's training. However, in later years, as a reward for her outstanding work, she was elected as a delegate to the XXIVth Party Congress of the CPSU.

THE INTEGRATIVE EFFORTS OF THE KOMSOMOL

A survey of the newspaper Sovetskaia molodezh' during the period of this study reveals a more sustained and systematic effort at integrating Latvians in the sphere of labor and education than that recorded in Sovetskaia Latviia. In addition to the competition with forces for Latvian nationality consciousness, the Komsomol paper promotes interrepublic integration in the Soviet West. The integrative efforts are not merely confined to the processes of industrial production. Rather, they are more universal, for they encompass the cultural and social as well as the political and economic spheres of group interaction.

The Komsomol's efforts in interrepublic integration are supported by a well-defined program that outlines the necessary conditions to achieve such integration. The Komsomol program is the only concerted, organized effort in the competition between nationality divisiveness and integration that has emerged in the Latvian press. Sovetskaia molodezh' presents the program in some detail in an article covering the Union-wide Komsomol meeting held on December 25-26, 1972.

The theme of this conference, "With Intensive Work and Study We Will Mark the Decisive Year of the Five-Year Plan," encompasses the two major realms of societal integration upon which the Komsomol directs its efforts—the enterprise and the educational system. Conference resolutions emphasized that the "Komsomol organization in industry, construction, transport, the kolkhozy and sovkhozy, scientific research, and trade will work out measures for socialist competition among the Komsomol and youth in 1973, the decisive year of the ninth Five-Year Plan."[26]

The Komsomol program is enunciated in the following passage from Sovetskaia molodezh':

> The primary attention in socialist commitment—fulfillment and over-fulfillment of the plan—is the introduction of new techniques and technology, strengthening the role of economics, the growth of general educational knowledge, higher qualifications and discipline in work. . . . The duty of the Komsomol organizations in educational institutions is to determine the problems of university students and pupils in their achieving a deeper and more exact knowledge, to heighten their ideological political level, their active participation in scientific-technical innovations and in socially useful labor.[27]

Guided by that program, Komsomol efforts for societal integration in Soviet Latvia are channeled into three major areas of activity: the personal example set by a Komsomol member before his peers; influencing pupils enrolled in vocational colleges; and the increased interaction among "Brother Republics" of the Soviet West.

Countless articles appear in Sovietskaia molodezh' extolling the accomplishments in study and work of the individual Komsomol member. Often, these profiles are supplemented by articles describing the achievements of all Komsomol-directed personnel in the enterprise. Though many letters from such personnel are printed in Sovetskaia molodezh', only one statement of this type appeared in Sovetskaia Latviia during the period under review.

The exemplary attitude and work of a Komsomol member frequently becomes a topic of discussion in the Komsomol press. The close bonds between labor and education are clearly delineated in a brief sketch of the life of a Komsomol girl, Vaira Dambe, of the Olaine sovkhoz. The daughter of a peasant family, she entered the Ekabpilaskii Agricultural Tekhnikum immediately following her graduation from the eight-year school system. After five years of combined study and work on the sovkhoz, she graduated from the evening course. As a young technician she traveled to various kolkhozy and sovkhozy of the Republic until receiving her appointment as accountant for the Olaine sovkhoz. Subsequently elected secretary of the Komsomol organization, the young woman is presently studying for the preparatory courses of the Latvian Agricultural Academy.[28]

Many statements coming from organizations link economic achievements with a more general prosperity. Yet, the Komsomol organization remains central to these achievements. A young agricultural economist and secretary of the Komsomol organization of a kolkhoz in the Elgaskii region writes to Sovetskaia molodezh':

> I am very proud of the success we achieved this year through extraordinary labor. . . . We don't have many Komsomol members among us, twenty persons in all—mechanics, livestock workers and teachers. It is difficult to work, to try to do everything at once. [But] we have a unified organization. The Komsomol and the young workers have their share in this success.
> Contemporary agriculture requires specialization. The Komsomol organization of the kolkhoz conducts a great deal of work among the youth for raising the general educational level.
> At present, within the organization there are five people with higher education, seven with specializations from secondary schools and nine are enrolled in the XIth course at evening school.[29]

The bonds between the Komsomol organization, labor productivity, and education are reaffirmed. The Komsomol becomes the decisive instrument of labor productivity. Although in that instance there were only 20 Komsomol members involved, the unity of the organization is said to have facilitated the success in production. Note also the separation between the Komsomol and other youthful laborers of the kolkhoz—"The Komsomol and the young workers have their share in this success."

A second major area of concern for the Komsomol is the vocational college which provides secondary school pupils with both a general education and a job specialization. Latvian educators and managers of enterprises have also expressed great interest in the vocational college. After the completion of the eighth grade, the pupil enters the industrial enterprise which complements his chosen skill; he then enrolls in the ninth and tenth grades of general education at an evening or shift school.[30]

As the vocational colleges encourage the enrollment of young Latvians, the Republic's Komsomol organization has, in turn, taken great interest in every aspect of vocational education. In fact, Sovetskaia molodezh' provided a more complete set of statistics regarding the professional technical college than either Sovetskaia Latviia or the 1971 statistical handbook for education, published in Moscow in 1971.[31]

According to Sovetskaia molodezh', Latvia's State Committee of the Soviet Ministry for Vocational Education presently directs 67 colleges. Current enrollment numbers 25,000 pupils, and in previous years approximately 200,000 Latvian workers have been trained by the vocational institutions.[32]

At present, every fourth skilled worker in the Republic has graduated from the vocational school system. Approximately one-third of these graduates will receive a higher job classification than fellow laborers graduated from general secondary schools. By 1975, Latvia will boast an additional 38 vocational schools.[33]

To emphasize further the importance of these institutions for the Latvian economy, the Komsomol press quotes A. E. Voss, First Secretary of the Latvian Communist party:

> The basic foundry of young working cadres has become the system of vocational education. . . . The Party emphasizes the need to broaden and strengthen the network of secondary vocational colleges, [for] they will fully answer the demands of scientific-technical progress and will give the rich experience of general education to the individual. . . . The upbringing of the young and their vocational education . . . must be placed under the direction of the Party, the soviet, the Komsomol, and other societal organizations.[34]

Voss elucidates a central concern regarding the vocational training programs. The one-to-two year training period within the vocational college does not lend itself to the traditional Party responsibility for the upbringing of the young. Therefore, it is thought essential that well-organized Komsomol units be formed within the colleges, for in this manner the Komsomol member can influence his peers. Immediately following Voss's statement in Sovetskaia molodezh' appears a description of several of the best Komsomol organizations within vocational colleges. It is notable that the two colleges mentioned are directly connected to neighboring factories—via the Komsomol organization. Thus, "a close friendship has been established between the Komsomol Organization of Technical College No. 6 and the firm 'Latvia'." And in the Daugavpilsk Vocational College No. 1, students who are members of the Lenin Komsomol of the college learn industrial methods from "Heroes of Socialist Labor" in the local chemical fiber plant.[35]

Young Latvians having reached the ages of 16 or 17 are thus being actively recruited for work in enterprises. The Komsomol, with its firm commitment to educational excellence, provides the inducement to them of availability of higher educational programs and job promotion.

Examples of the outstanding skilled worker and student abound in the Komsomol press, and, in every instance, their sterling qualities are linked with some kind of larger group. For example, a recent sociological survey outlined the attitudes of outstanding young engineers employed in Latvian industry. The qualities that these professionals valued most highly were "patriotism, love of one's occupation, ability to live within the group, independent judgment and consciousness of one's societal debt."[36]

Within the secondary schools of the Republic, pupils were faced with the question "How does one become an honors student?" Ilona Kalova, an honors pupil in the ninth grade of the Second Middle (Secondary) School of Rezeken gave the typical response:

> During Komsomol meetings [conducted in the course of the school year] serious discussions ensued concerning the fact that Komsomol plays a great part in educating young people. . . . The Komsomol [insures] that pupils take part in . . . mutual aid groups, consultation circles and clubs.[37]

Tenth grade student Sergei Shishkin at the 48th Secondary School in Riga, further defined the role of the Komsomol within the school: "The social view of knowledge—this is new in the work of the Komsomol organization. The [Komsomol's] goals are to deepen knowledge of the foundations of science and to strengthen the popularity of knowledge and the handing down of this knowledge to younger comrades."[38]

The final area of Komsomol concern is said to be the increasing of interaction among the "Brother Republics" in the Soviet West. During the 1972 jubilee year, Sovetskaia molodezh' devoted all of the Sunday editions to news of other republics. During November and December 1972, Moldavia, Lithuania, and Estonia were featured in special issues. These editions covered all aspects of potential integration—political, economic, cultural, and linguistic—and proved to be the most comprehensive press effort openly advocating integration within the Soviet West discovered during 1972-73.

These reports are mainly descriptive, their purpose being to acquaint young Latvians with prominent features of their "Brother Republics." However, articles describing industrial output stress the connections between Latvian industries and those of other republics. The special issue devoted to Moldavia systematically outlined the flow of goods between Latvia and that republic.[39]

In the Lithuanian edition, ties between the Komsomol organizations of Latvia and Lithuania were emphasized in several articles. The Lithuanian Komsomol states that it had "especially strong ties"

with the Komsomol organizations of the other Baltic republics, and
in particular with the Latvian Komsomol. Numerous members of the
Latvian Komsomol are reported to be studying in "zone schools" for
Komsomol activities located in Vilnius, and in turn, Lithuanian Kom-
somol members are encouraged to attend similar institutions in
Latvia.[40]

CONCLUSIONS AND IMPLICATIONS

Mutual assistance and support may well provide the keystone
of integrative efforts within the Latvian SSR. Given Latvia's firm
commitment to and great pride in the Republic's economy, it follows
that much nationality perseverance has been invested in this sphere.
This is precisely the area upon which efforts for integrating Latvia
into the pattern of the Soviet Western republics have been most consistently focused.

Regional economic integration is gaining greater importance
in present-day efforts at equitable economic development. Both the
developed and the developing worlds and the socialist and capitalist
economies have moved in this direction. From all indications in the
Latvian press, it is evident that these efforts have their parallels
in Latvia. If present efforts for economic integration continue in their
scope and intensity, Latvia will move inexorably toward greater economic and social integration within the Soviet West and the USSR as
a whole. And subsequently, the vast reserves of Latvian national
pride and effort in its industrial sphere will have to find a new
accommodation with such integration or be subsumed under greater
societal goals in the construction of a Soviet socialist economy.

The Latvian Komsomol provides the greatest support for this
kind of economic integration of the Latvian SSR. Of all the forces for
integration yet described, the Komsomol alone consciously and systematically directs its efforts toward facilitating the integration of
Latvian society with the broader Soviet sphere. Through a well-defined
program and clearly ordered priorities, the Komsomol applies its
efforts to the major areas of potential societal integration in Latvia—
the economic enterprise and the educational system.

In this way, groups which augment Latvian nationality consciousness compete with advocates of integration for the loyalty of
youthful Latvian workers and students. This competition has been
amply substantiated by the Latvian Party daily and Komsomol press.
It appears likely that the response of the younger generation to these
overtures (provided they do respond, for the press gives little indication of the real attitudes of Latvian youth) will be in the direction of
increased integration into Soviet society. The Komsomol maintains

active programs within the enterprise and the school system to insure just such a response.

It appears, however, that as Latvia moves steadily toward greater economic and social cooperation with other Soviet Western republics, Latvian culture will remain untouched by efforts for integration. Latvia's propensity for noninteraction within the cultural field has thus far remained intact. Sovetskaia Latviia prints numerous articles about the Latvian arts, and these arts remain purely Latvian with no reference to the cultural achievements of other nationalities. In this manner, Latvian culture may well prove to be the most enduring symbol of the Republic's nationality consciousness, and at least during the present generation, Latvia will retain its cultural integrity even as it becomes socially and economically integrated with other Soviet republics.

Thus, inside the larger framework of group interactions within the Soviet West, Latvian socioeconomic and cultural spheres tend to diverge. The socioeconomic sector embraces a mutitude of interactions between forces for integration and those for national divisiveness, whereas the Latvian culture has not yet yielded to such intensive pressures. However, should the more broadly-based and organized efforts of the Komsomol prove successful, the present generation of Latvian youth may give ground before pressures for cultural integration.

Both the nature and scope of changes occurring recently within the Latvian SSR have significantly redefined the concept and the reality of Latvian nationality. Intense Soviet efforts for economic and social integration are moving Latvia toward more frequent interaction with its counterparts in the Soviet West. Thus, despite its independence and competence within these spheres, Latvia is steadily relinquishing more autonomy in favor of cooperative ventures with neighboring republics. At this level of interaction, therefore, Latvia has begun to contribute to greater unity within the Soviet West.

The Latvian press, habitually emphasizing the industrial sector, provides an important forum for the discussion of these integrative ideals. It additionally serves as one important link between the policy outlines drawn up in Party, Komsomol, labor union conferences and governing bodies, and the application of these policies within the enterprise and the school.

Similar efforts are no doubt being conducted within other republics of the Soviet West to encourage nationality consciousness as such to flourish while certain aspects of nationality divisiveness—its concrete manifestations within economic and social fields especially—are subject to increasing interaction with integrative forces. The intensity of these interactions, as measured by their frequency of occurrence reported in the local press and other sources, portends a greater movement toward cooperation and further integration within the Soviet West.

In this way Latvia provides an important case study for the investigation of the nationality question in the Soviet West. But even more important, Latvia may also assume the role of a focal point from which to generalize developments concerning the nationality question. The interaction of competing groups seeking to dominate societal institutions may be projected to the entire area of the Soviet West. Soviet efforts to subordinate nationality to economic and social goals constitutes a major trend, both at the present time and perhaps for the immediate future, within the Latvian Republic and the Soviet West. The nationality question then remains an issue of vital importance for Latvia and its neighboring republics of the Soviet West. Consequently, the near future will probably be characterized by the intense activity of both divisive-minded and integrative groups as these forces each seek to resolve the contest in their favor.

NOTES

1. Algirdas Landsbergis, "The Baltic Republics: Cohesion and Division" (Lecture delivered to Seminar on Soviet Nationality Problems, Columbia University, September 26, 1972).

2. Rein Taagepera, "Dissimilarities Among the Northwest Soviet Republics," in A. Ziedonis, et al., eds., Problems of Mini-Nations: Baltic Perspectives (San Jose, Calif.: Association for the Advancement of Baltic Studies, 1973).

3. Ibid., p. 3.

4. Landsbergis, "Cohesion and Divison."

5. Stephen P. Dunn, Cultural Processes in the Baltic Area Under Soviet Rule (Research Series, No. 11, Institute of International Studies, University of California, Berkeley, 1966) pp. 34-35.

6. Ibid., p. 34.

7. Lithuania, Latvia, Estonia: 1965-1970-1975. (No publication date). Pamphlet obtained at the Soviet Mission to the United Nations, New York, 1972).

8. Narodnoe khoziaistvo SSSR v 1969 g. (Moscow: Statistika, 1971), p. 25.

9. Charlotte Saikowski, "Riga's Fascination Widely Appreciated," The Christian Science Monitor, September 12, 1969, p. 17.

10. "Latvians Chided for Nationalism," New York Times, March 21, 1971, p. 17.

11. Narodnoe khoziaistvo SSSR v 1969 g. (Moscow: Statistika, 1970), pp. 34-35.

12. Saikowski, p. 17.

13. "Latvians Chided for Nationalism," p. 17.

14. Bernard Gwertzman, "Latvian Protest Held Authentic," New York Times, February 27, 1972, p. 11.

15. E. Trofimova, "Viktoriia na tranzistorakh," Sovetskaia Latviia, November 14, 1972, p. 2.

16. Sovetskaia Latviia, (Untitled article; author unsigned), January 1, 1973, p. 3.

17. L. Kurdiumov, "Na pervom etape," Sovetskaia Latviia, November 14, 1972, pp. 2-3.

18. Ibid., pp. 2-3.

19. M. Priezhkalnen', "Krupneishaia v respublike," Sovetskaia Latviia, November 14, 1972, p. 2.

20. K. Mulin, "Za iubilieniyi pochetnyi znak," Sovetskaia Latviia, December 11, 1972, p. 1.

21. Ibid., p. 1.

22. A. Beliaev, "Chetkii rutm, otlichnoe kachestvo," Sovetskaia Latviia, November 2, 1972, p. 1.

23. Ibid., p. 1.

24. D. Proskurovskii, "K vseobshchemy srednemy-profilaktika otseva," Sovetskaia Latviia, November 15, 1972, p. 2.

25. L. Prokof'eva, "Doroga vverkh," Sovetskaia Latviia, January 1, 1973.

26. "Postavlenie biuro Ts. K.V.L.S.M. o vsesoiuznom komsomol'-skom sobranii 'udarnym trudom i otlichnoi ucheboi oznamenuem reshaiushchii god piatiletkil," Sovetskaia molodezh', December 17, 1972, p. 3.

27. Ibid. p. 3.

28. Sovetskaia molodezh', (Untitled article; author unsigned), December 20, 1972, p. 3.

29. A. Rudin, "Komsomolets ne podvedu," Sovetzkaia Latviia, February 17, 1972, p. 1.

30. S. Ia. Batyshev, "Razvitie professional'no teknichiskogo obrazovaniia v SSR," Sovetskaia pedagogika, VIII (August 1972), p. 53.

31. Narodnoe obrazovanie, nauka i kul'tura v SSR (Moscow: "Statistika," 1971).

31. "Rabochemy klassu-dostoinoe popolnenie," Sovetskaia molodezh', November 17, 1972, p. 1.

33. Ibid.

34. Ibid.

35. Ibid.

36. "G. Kerezhina, "Ekzamen na vsiu zhizn'," Sovetskaia molodezh', January 5, 1973, p. 3.

37. "Kak Stat' Otlichnikom?" Sovetskaia molodezh', January 5, 1973, p. 3.

38. Ibid.

39. See Sovetskaia molodezh', November 12, 26, 1972, and December 10, 1972.

40. M. Irinina, "I ia nogy gordit'sa," Sovetskaia molodezh', November 26, 1972, p. 3.

7

PARTY RESPONSE TO
LITHUANIAN UNREST
Emmett George

     Events within the recent past indicate that nationality conscious-
ness remains a significant force among Lithuanians, and that the role
played by the Roman Catholic Church, although not overtly anti-
Soviet, in effect reinforces this nationality consciousness. The
hypothesis of this chapter is that Lithuanian Communist party and
Komsomol authorities desire to minimize this nationality consciousness by pressuring educational institutions within the Republic to
heighten the ideological awareness of students and workers. The
government's emphasis upon ideological and technical expertise is
intended in part to channel the energies of discontented Lithuanians
away from expressing dissatisfaction through nationalistic urges.
Thus, Party officials are apparently attempting to promote greater
involvement in political and economic activities. This desired involvement in economic development (such as participation in the fulfillment of economic plans), is expected to reduce the effects of nationalism, which is partly based upon religion. Further, the authorities
evidently believe that a populace armed with the "correct" ideological
and technical preparation is better equipped for participation in the
economy of the Republic and the USSR.
     Within a spectrum of complex relationships, both within the
Republic and involving Lithuania's Baltic neighbors, this study focuses
upon the interaction of Communist party authorities of Lithuania with
the educational institutions. This interaction mainly takes the form
of ideological campaigns that are apparently intended to mitigate the
spread of religiously-based nationalism. In the case of Lithuania,
we are presented with a unique opportunity to examine Party interaction with other sectors of society in response to violent, well-
publicized resistance to Soviet authority, namely, the disturbances
of May 1972, that occurred in Kaunas and other Lithuanian cities.
We will assume, therefore, that Party and government interaction

with the educational system takes the form of ideological and technical preparation, and we will hypothesize that this interaction increased in intensity as a result of the Lithuanian riots. This is not to suggest that the increased emphasis upon ideological and professional training was the only response on the part of the Soviet Lithuanian authorities to the unsettling disturbances; indeed, our evidence revealed that heightened attention given to Lithuanian cultural activities may also have served as an "escape valve" for nationalist emotions.

In order to obtain evidence for this hypothesized reemphasis of ideology, a detailed survey was made of the major daily Russian-language newspaper of the Lithuanian SSR, Sovetskaia Litva, for a six-month period following the riots. In order to establish a basis for comparison, a study of the press for a five-month period preceding the riots was also undertaken.

It was hoped that by establishing what could be considered a "normal" period of official Soviet press coverage and content, analogies could be drawn as to the extent of reaction to the unrest. Special regard was given to the fact that the preriot period was marked by preparations for the start of the 1972-73 school year, inasmuch as this inquiry specifically concerns ideological interaction in education.

RELIGIOUS AND SECULAR DISSENT
IN LITHUANIA

On November 23, 1970, perhaps the first signal of unrest and discontent with Soviet administration in Lithuania was sounded when Simas Kudirka, a sailor, defected from his vessel, the Sovetskaia Litva, to a U.S. Coast Guard cutter off Martha's Vineyard. The 42-year-old Kudirka, a radio operator, was returned after ten hours to the Soviet vessel where he was reportedly beaten and placed under arrest. At his trial in May 1971, when asked if he considered his act a betrayal of his country, the sailor said: "I did not betray my homeland, Lithuania. . . . I did not consider Russia, which is called the Soviet Union today, to be my motherland."[1] Speaking further in his defense, Kudirka was quoted as saying: "There is no true socialism in Lithuania at all—only a parody of socialism."[2] Kudirka was sentenced to ten years in prison on May 17, 1971.

This incident may be symptomatic of a broader current of discontent in Lithuania, the principal aspect of which involves the Roman Catholic Church. The question of religious unrest in the Lithuanian SSR and the historic impact of Catholicism upon nationality consciousness were of major importance in this research. Students of Lithuanian affairs have long been aware of the impact of the Roman Catholic religion upon Lithuanian society, and of the efforts of Soviet authorities to draw attention away from the Church. These efforts, as illustrated in the series of complaints about religious harassment that are detailed below, seem to suggest that the official policy of treating religiously-based nationalism made many Lithuanians more sympathetic to the plight of the believers. An analysis of dissident literature for the period in advance of the May riots indicates that religious dissatisfaction had reached a very high level of intensity.

Evidence of this discontent is contained in the Chronicle of Current Events, a samizdat publication, which began appearing in Lithuania in early 1968, and which was recently spirited out and received by emigre sources in the West.[3] These documents, as they pertain to Lithuania, concerned themselves overwhelmingly with the struggle for religious rights by Roman Catholics. Almost no information is presented in these sources as to the existence of other forms of discontent. For example, a year after the Kudirka affair, about 2,000 Catholics of Prenai Parish, 20 miles south of Kaunas, reportedly sent an open letter to Soviet authorities charging that freedom of religion was being curbed by the local officials.[4] The Lithuanian parishioners had contended that priests were being arrested for administering religious rites to children.

In Varena Raion, a month later, parents of Valkinikai Parish appealed to local authorities, alleging that their children had been discriminated against because of religious beliefs.[5] The parents reported that their children were interrogated in public schools about their suspected church attendance. The children were told their conduct grades would be lowered and the church-going would be noted on their records. It was reported that the children received criticism from other students, which included the appearance of cartoons in wall newspapers ridiculing the young Catholics, and personal lectures from Komsomol and other student groups.

In recent months, Catholics have reportedly been gathering petitions among believers in rural parishes. In one such case, over 17,000 signatures were collected and sent to General Secretary of the Communist Party of the Soviet Union (CPSU) Leonid Brezhnev, Secretary General of the United Nations Kurt Waldheim, and to a number of Soviet Lithuanian authorities.[6]

There have been at least seven cases reported in which priests were jailed or released from their duties for allegedly teaching religion to children or for administering religious rites. In one of the most significant cases of this kind in December 1971, 47 priests of the Vilnius archdiocese addressed a statement to the General Secretary of the CPSU and to the Council of Ministers of the USSR demanding various religious freedoms. During that same month, another memorandum reportedly signed by 17,059 Catholics was sent to Brezhnev and, a month later, to Waldheim.[7] Both petitions underscored continued violations of the rights of religious believers. They also maintained that priests had been imprisoned or exiled, that Catholic children were compelled to study atheism, that Party control of the theological seminary in Kaunas had caused a shortage in the number of priests, and that Catholics had been denied permission to construct or repair churches.[8]

On March 19, 1972, some 3,023 Catholics from the City of Klaipeda sent their appeal to Brezhnev for the return of a new church building that they claimed was closed during the Khrushchev period.[9] As is evident from these and other protests cited by Western sources, the disturbances that form the basis of this study were grounded firmly in religious discontent within the Republic.

Although evidence that directly demonstrates that Party and Komsomol authorities are uneasy about nationalistic tensions are generally lacking, the summer riots in Kaunas and other cities of the Lithuanian Republic demonstrate emphatically that nationality consciousness is indeed very strong. During the days of strife, May 14-15, 1972, a 20-year-old man, Roman Kalanta, reportedly poured gasoline over his clothing and burned himself to death.[10] Kalanta, a Catholic, was believed to have acted in protest against what emigre sources have termed the lack of religious freedom in the Lithuanian SSR. A policeman was reportedly killed and an estimated 200 demonstrators arrested when police and paratroops garrisoned nearby were dispatched to quell the disturbances. The official statement concerning the Kaunas unrest, presented at a Moscow news conference, held that Kalanta was mentally disturbed, and that tensions within the Lithuanian SSR were sponsored by "a small group of hooligans" and local criminal elements.[11] On September 25, the Soviet news agency, TASS, reported on the eve of the trial of eight suspected leaders that, "most of the accused had been in a state of heavy intoxication" at the time of the riots. The agency also claimed that two of the men had previous arrest records.[12]

Kalanta's suicide triggered several other protest actions, including a petition signed by 300 Lithuanians, reportedly presented to President Nixon during the Moscow summit meeting in May 1972, and a second self-immolation, by V. Stonis, age 23, in Varena on May 18, 1972.[13] This was followed by still a third self-immolation on June 3, 1972, in Siauliai, this time of a 60-year-old Catholic, K. Andriuskevicius.[14]

The American Lithuanian emigre newsletter ELTA reported: "In an aftermath of the Kaunas freedom riots, some 200 students were reported to have been arrested in Vilnius, capital of Lithuania, during June 11 through the 18th. They staged an anti-Soviet demonstration at the international handball games, distributed anti-regime leaflets, and hung the flags of independent Lithuania in the streets."[15]

These events evolved at a time when the Soviet socialist republics were actively preparing to celebrate the fiftieth anniversary of the founding of the USSR, a holiday designed to portray the Soviet system as a harmonious model to be emulated by multiethnic states. Therefore, it came as no surprise that the official Russian-language newspaper made little mention of these embarrassing events.

The survey of the Soviet Lithuanian press undertaken for this study revealed that although there was a definite and recurring emphasis on the reintensification of political studies following the May riots, the cultural calendar supplied the needed channels into which nationality discontent was initially diverted. A series of important cultural events, planned to begin May 23, probably hastened Lithuania's return to normalcy by occupying potential dissidents. For instance, some 4,000 choral performers gathered in the main square of Vilnius to perform in the first of a series of culture fests designed to further advance the objectives of the fiftieth anniversary.[16] This momentum reportedly spread to Kaunas with the Eighth Annual Holiday of Spring Poetry, which sought to honor famous Lithuanian poets of the past.[17]

However, the abundance of reports stressing a reemphasis on ideological preparation of future cadres was clearly the most dominant theme in the months that followed the disturbances.

The Catholic Church in Lithuania occupies a sensitive position in relation to the Soviet government. Lithuania is a relatively recent addition to the Soviet Union, and, as such, like the Western Ukraine, has a rich religious heritage.[18] Through its display of spiritual vitality, Lithuania offers a distinct contrast to some other republics of the USSR where religion is apparently under more rigid controls. The antireligious campaign of the mid-1960s, for example, closed about half of the existing Orthodox churches, but did not have a comparable effect upon Lithuanian Catholicism.[19] Although subjected to pressures and losses of personnel, the Church benefits from the solidarity of local clergy (as is evident by the letters and petitions detailed above that were sent to Soviet officials).

Despite obvious pressures and a competing ideology, the Catholic religion still retains much of its traditional influence upon Lithuanian social institutions.[20] On the specific question of combatting religious expression in Lithuania, only one directive was evident in the Soviet Lithuanian press on this subject during the period under study. In a speech given by V. Morkunas, First Secretary of the Central Committee of the Lithuanian Komsomol, the problem of the role of youth in fighting secretive religious expression was raised. Morkunas noted that although the number of church-goers had declined in recent years, young people continued to be ordained, and antireligious tactics were in need of improvement.[21]

THE IDEOLOGICAL PREPARATION OF
CADRES: A COUNTERMEASURE

The Party and Komsomol response to religious sympathies, judging from the official press, consisted of the presentation of an ideological challenge to both the formal and informal educational institutions of the Lithuanian SSR. Although there was only the single direct reference to religion, the campaign was seemingly aimed at reasserting the proper disciplinary controls and providing an attractive alternative to challenge traditional religious involvement.

The theme of increased ideological preparation of cadres was linked to a corresponding emphasis upon training in Marxist economics. Evidence of this second emphasis centers around comments made by A. Barkauskas, Secretary of the Central Committee of the Lithuanian Communist Party. Barkauskas stated that: "The institutions of higher education are called upon to prepare developed, ideologically well-rounded, mature young specialists . . . capable of carrying on discourse with the collectives."[22] Barkauskas, speaking before a group of Komsomol functionaries, trade unionists, and scholars, predicted that by the time the Ninth Five Year Plan is concluded, 140,000 such specialists will have been trained. It was also announced at the meeting held in Vilnius that salary increases for instructors and higher student stipends had been decreed. Additional support for the premise that Party and Komsomol officials are pressuring educational institutions to assume greater responsibilities for raising the ideological consciousness of cadres was supplied by the Sixth Plenum of the Central Committee of the Lithuanian Communist Party (July 6, 1972). Plenum leaders reportedly called on Party functionaries to intensify their personal attacks on "lesser forms of propaganda."[23] These lesser philosophies or forms of propaganda were said to include individualism and localism. Finally, the report of the plenum said that in preparation for the fiftieth anniversary of the USSR, Party and Komsomol cadres should seek to expose those elements of Lithuanian society "shielding liberalism" and the so-called apologists for imperialism.[24] The article charged that bourgeois propaganda was attempting to undermine the ideological commitments of the Soviet people.

In the days that immediately followed the riots, a variety of articles of ideological and economic importance were published in the official press. On May 17, 1972, in what appeared to signal a reduction in tensions, the plenum of the Vilnius City Committee of the Lithuanian Communist party met for the purpose of discussing questions pertaining to achieving universal secondary education of youth.[25] The Soviet Lithuanian news agency, ELTA*, published comments made by A. Umbrasas, Secretary of the Vilnius City Committee, claiming that some 3,500 teachers were involved in studying how best to achieve the goal of universal secondary education. It was also mentioned, however, that sound theoretical as well as practical skills were to be implanted.

The importance of theoretical or ideological training was emphasized once again in a directive that called for the improvement of the economic studies of cadres and praised the school for devoting more attention to the study of "the question of economic theory and politics of our party in accord with the resolutions of the XXIV Congress of the CPSU."[26] The report cautioned, however, that there were deficiencies in conducting economic studies. For example, it was stated that the Vilnius Raion Executive Committee had recently underscored shortcomings of workers under its supervision in theoretical seminars in the management of agriculture. The report also stated that Vilnius State University was in the process of creating a "permanent seminar" dealing with problems in economics. Also, the society "Knowledge" (Znanie) had reportedly decided to open lectures on economics in Vilnius, Kaunas, Klaipeda, Alilyce and other towns.

In keeping with this dual emphasis upon political economics and political-theoretical training of cadres, a Soviet author wrote a fairly lengthy account of the history of the school of basic Marxism-Leninism, attached to a Vilnius radio factory.[27] The writer praised one course in particular: "The International position of the USSR and the Foreign Policy of the CPSU," stating that the selection of this course was not accidental, in that it was designed to impart an understanding of the "strategy and tactics of class struggle of the proletariat" and the importance of certain international developments, including agreements signed between the USSR and USA. This pressure for political and ideological training was supported by A. Iakniunene, Director of the Institute for Political Education of Anikshchiaisky District of the Lithuanian CP: "Our Party always shows great concern over the Marxist-Leninist education of Communists. Of all cadres last year in Anikshchiaisky Raion, a sound education was given to over 2,500 persons; of these two-thirds were Communists."[28]

Speaking at the concluding sessions of the Sixth Plenum of the Central Committee of the Lithuanian Communist Party in Vilnius on June 3, 1972, A. Sneckus, the First Secretary, proclaimed that the annual exchange of Party documents and Party cards was not merely a mechanical act,"not simply the exchange of old Party documents

---

*Not to be confused with the emigre newsletter.

for new ones."29 The 70-year-old Party chief explained that the
annual event had a greater meaning and political significance, namely,
its importance in raising the effectiveness of Party organizations.
Sneckus cautioned that it would be to "the great misfortune of everyone if Party and candidate-members allow a lapse in State discipline."
Charging that Party organizations were not taking sufficient steps
to oversee the supervision of collectives, Sneckus said, "The fight
against the spread of localism . . . in our society, must be given the
center of attention. . . ."30

Sneckus' statement at the concluding session of the Sixth Plenum
seemed to set the stage for the publication of a variety of reports
that dealt specifically with the subject of discipline. On September
15, I. Marsheshayskene, Chairman of the Poljeski district People's
Control Committee, in summarizing the past achievements of con-
trollers in the Lithuanian SSR, said that the need still existed to continue supervision and checks of all areas of the Republic's activities.31
A week later a Union-wide directive was issued, entitled: "Education
in the Heroic Tradition," which echoed the official Soviet position
on the subject of discipline. In addition to demanding greater participation in plan fulfillment and in the preparation for the national holiday,
the report articulated the concern of the XXIV Party Congress for
the education of the Soviet people, through a respect for achievements
of the motherland. Party organizations, it was said, "should give
considerably more attention to the patriotic education of the working
class."32

On September 29, 1972, an evaluation of the work of the Marxist-
Leninist Evening Universities was undertaken. Established in Vilnius,
Kaunas, and Klaipeda, some 3,000 persons were studying in these
institutions. L. Vitalis, director of the Vilnius branch, said that
about 1,400 students were studying such subjects as economic theory,
Party politics, and production management.33 A day later a related
article was published by the Eighth Plenary Session of the Vilnius
Committee. Participants at the Plenum again underscored the problem
of Marxist-Leninist study and of improving the quality of economic
education of supervisory cadres.34

With the start of the 1972-73 school year, the formal educational
institutions of the Lithuanian SSR assumed responsibility for continuing
the pressure for increased ideological consciousness among students
and workers. The evidence that follows, extracted from the Soviet
press, leaves little doubt that ideological themes were the most
dominant in the press and constituted a major preoccupation of Party
and Komsomol authorities. On September 5, K. Zhukauskas, Deputy
Minister of Higher and Secondary Special Education of the Lithuanian
SSR, said in an interview with a Sovetskaya Litva correspondent that
Lithuanian institutions of higher education (VUZ) will be confronted

with the tasks of promoting "an increased level of preparation and ideological-political education of future specialists."[35] Concerning the new school year, Zhukauskas explained that higher educational institutions in Lithuania were expected to open their doors to 60,000 students (an estimated increase of 5,000 over 1970).[36] This increase in enrollments would make direction of activities for cadres more difficult, Zhukauskas concluded.

According to a report published on October 20, 1972, an estimated 30,000 students were studying in Vilnius higher schools, of which 12,000 were said to be Komsomol members.[37] Commenting further on this situation, V. Koiala, secretary to the City Party Committee, charged VUZ with the immediate task of shaping the convictions of its students, and stressed the importance of contacts among teachers, Party and Komsomol members, and youth.[38]

The set of directives presented above are systematic responses to a Union-wide decree, "On Measures for Future Improvement of Higher Education in the Country," published on July 30, 1972. This directive seemed to have triggered a variety of official responses which serve to build the case for ideological intensification. A certain number of ideological articles normally accompany the start of new school years in the USSR. But for the period covered by this study, the subject thoroughly dominated the Russian-language press of Lithuania. The Marxist-Leninist Evening Universities, for example, were said to be providing information in economic theory, Party politics, and production management to about 3,000 students, according to the director of the Vilnius branch.[39]

On October 7, Sovetskaia Litva underscored the importance of evening university facilities in Vilnius.[40] Praise was given to the seminar-type atmosphere which provided instruction in problems of economics, management, and the scientific organization of labor. The facility was reportedly in the process of turning out better propagandists (students and teachers) for service to Lithuania, according to the school's director, A. Pashtukas. In addition to higher economic studies, the system of Marxist-Leninist evening schools has increased discipline and responsibility for instructional activities in the Lithuanian SSR.

An analysis of the fall months (1972) of the Lithuanian press indicates that the ideological campaign was directed mainly at the higher education institutions, political study facilities, and adult evening study groups. The reported ages of the arrested demonstrators (young adults) in connection with the May riots (1972), indicated that these initiatives stressing greater ideological awareness, were directed particularly at that age group.[41] Greater activism in the area of political study might be intended to detract from other activities, such as religion.

During the months preceding the riots the ideological content
of Sovetskaia Litva was basically the same as during the aftermath
of the May disturbances. The Party and Komsomol promoted such
activities as military-patriotic training, greater responsibility of
supervisory cadres, and the need for economic integration with other
republics of the USSR. Supervisory cadres of the Lithuanian Republic
were given directives from the Central Committee of the CPSU,
urging them to take a more active role in Party organizational work,
and to intensify their study of the theories of Marxism-Leninism
and national Party politics. Another example from this period involved an assessment of "patriotic education" of students in the
vocational schools of Panevezhisa District.[42] It was reported that
evening youth studies had been organized with the participation of
veteran workers of industrial and agricultural enterprises. Finally,
on April 11, it was claimed that over 150,000 Communists, Komsomol
youths, and non-Party activists of Lithuania were working on developing the system of Party and Communist political education in
Lithuania.[43]

The evidence cited above suggests that there was no discernible
change in press content after the May riots. Essentially, the difference was in the quantity and length of the reports. Although the preriot period, as stated, was heavy in ideological expression, the period
that followed the May outbreaks was completely dominated by such
materials.

Another channel into which nationality perseverance was continuously being diverted was the area of economic, technical,
and cultural cooperation with Lithuania's Baltic neighbors and the
other regions of the USSR. Systematically, Party and Komsomol
authorities, through their exercise of power, were striving to keep
the energies of potential dissidents flowing into these prescribed
channels. For example, Lithuanians were frequently told that it was
only through this unified family of republics that the Lithuanian SSR
could flourish. According to N. Kobiuzev, an official of the Council
of Ministers of the Lithuanian SSR, economic growth since 1940 had
been due largely to the fact that the Lithuanian economy had been
supplemented by cooperation with other areas of the USSR. He cited,
for example, tractors, trucks, elevators and motorcycles imported
from Belorussia; washing machines and pumps received from Latvia;
excavators and electric motors from Estonia; and a variety of raw
materials and technology acquired from the Ukraine.[44]

Another example of "the fruits of friendship" was provided by
Iosif Manyushis, Chairman of the Council of Ministers of the Lithuanian SSR, in an article published for Western readers in the magazine
Soviet Life. Manyushis recalled that before World War II, Lithuania
lagged behind Latvia and Estonia in industrial growth, and suffered

from a high unemployment rate of 75,000. Since 1940, the Republic, shedding its largely agrarian character, has progressed primarily because of the exchange of specialists and economic cooperation with the Russian Federation, the Ukraine, Belorussia, Latvia, and Estonia.[45]

As further evidence of this attempt to cultivate a broader outlook among discontented Lithuanians, I. Bachilis, a former instructor at the Kaunas Polytechnical Institute, cited the high degree of cooperation among students at the institute. Bachilis said that in the different branches of the institute, students from many parts of the USSR including Estonians, Ukrainians, Jews, Poles, and Latvians, had come to study.[46]

The publication of a Baltic edition of the Soviet Journal Kommunist in July 1972, further illustrates the importance attached to Baltic cooperation. The journal, prepared by a Kommunist staff composed of Lithuanians, Latvians, and Estonians, was termed a Baltic contribution to preparations for the fiftieth anniversary celebration.[47] The special issue cover of the journal, "The Three Sisters," was reportedly designed by the Lithuanian artist, A. Skiruitite.

Regional cooperation is urged primarily because Lithuanians have a low rate of migration to areas outside of their republic.[48] This fact is no doubt important in explaining the pressure to broaden their political outlook. In 1970, Lithuanians in their own Republic comprised over 90 percent of the population, and relatively small numbers of non-Lithuanians resided in the Republic (268,000 Russians and 240,000 Poles are the only non-Lithuanian groups represented in significant numbers in Lithuania).[49] There is also a relatively low rate of Russian in-migration into the Republic. Furthermore, Lithuanians themselves can be found in substantial numbers in only one other republic of the Soviet West, Latvia, where some 41,000 presently live.

On the specific question of ideology, it remains unproven that advanced or semiadvanced Marxist-Leninist knowledge (ideology) can alter vocational and technical backwardness among unskilled workers. Furthermore, it is at best debatable whether ideological indoctrination alone can lead to the desired level of involvement in the economic sector. The absence of a comprehensive set of material incentives makes the success of this policy highly doubtful. Although economic studies are designed to supplement the emphasis on ideological study, Marxist-Leninist economics must be taught, out of necessity, with at least a token promise stating that material rewards will follow.

Party and Komsomol authorities, as the hypothesis of the study states, are attempting to make discontented Lithuanians more interested in Union-wide affairs. It is hoped these ideologically-trained cadres will develop an "internationalist view." Lithuanian Party chief Sneckus underscored the importance of greater participation in the national economy.[50] He explained that since the Republic's entry into the Soviet Union (1940), its economy has recorded noticeable gains, and he reemphasized the benefits of working in harmony and engaging in economic cooperation with other republics of the Soviet Union. As evident from this statement, the promise of greater economic participation is the most effective way of channeling or redirecting nationalistic urges.

Recent reports indicate that Lithuanians have a definite appetite for the fruits of economic development. Pravda charged that there were several cases of resort homes complete with saunas being built at public expense in the Lithuanian SSR for high officials, and operated at a financial loss.[51] These losses were allegedly covered up by hidden public subsidies. The saunas, opened by a small group of individuals, were only one part of the Soviet press attack that also condemned such things as bridge-playing, long hair, and other "bourgeois" cultural influences.

Evidence extracted from the September 1972, sampling of the local press indicated that efforts are being made to satisfy these obvious material cravings within the Lithuanian Republic. These efforts included advertisements for professional schools in Vilnius and Kedainski that offered technical instruction in both Russian and Lithuanian languages.[52] Two of the three advertisements referred only to courses being taught exclusively in the Russian language, while the other mentioned instruction being given in both languages. The advertisements may indicate that these courses are mainly aimed at Russians living in Lithuania, or they may illustrate the possible social and economic benefits attached to learning the Russian language.

Prior to the Soviet occupation of 1940, Lithuania was basically agricultural in orientation, and educational responsibilities were assigned mostly to Church-related private institutions. Although Soviet organizational efforts apparently reversed Lithuania's agricultural emphasis through the development of light industries, the Republic presently is at best 50 percent industrial in nature.[53] In light of this fact, the Soviets (Party and Komsomol officials) must deal decisively not only with the problem of religiously-based nationalism, but also with the problems related to modernizing the Republic.

Since the May riots of 1972, Party and Komsomol authorities have been attempting through their reemphasis upon ideological and technical expertise to bring about a greater involvement on the part of students and young workers in the business of modernization.

Officially, the reaction to the May events has been subdued and rather low-key. By not mentioning that the problem of religiously-based nationalism had assumed serious proportions, Party and

Komsomol leaders apparently hoped that through a natural evolution of events, coupled with the skillful use of propaganda, the problem would be resolved. Also, it was probably believed that greater involvement in economic and political pursuits promises to submerge potential dissidents deeper into the economic development process.

In Lithuania as well as in other Soviet republics, it appears from our evidence that social unrest or reassertions of nationality consciousness produce visible benefits in certain areas, including literature and economic development. Immediate official reaction to social deviance seemed to be characterized by a tightening of ideological and physical controls, but once Party authority was firmly reestablished, a period of liberalism in areas of literary expression ensued.

Reports bearing greater cultural significance began appearing toward the end of 1972; the most important of these being an article published in late January 1973. The occasion was the opening of a Republic-wide art exhibition, attended by some 200,000 persons. In honor of the occasion, Party Secretary Barkauskas proclaimed: "Literature and art in Lithuania is definitely free from national bias, narrow-mindedness and provincialism."[54] He added that art exhibitions of this type represent the creative efforts of the working people, whose path has been reshaped toward Communist construction. "The main concern of our artists must be with the investigation of personalities, new subjects and their revolutionary significance, always based on an analysis of the social structures of Soviet society," he continued. Ten days earlier at the opening of the Eighth Meeting of Lithuanian Artists this "saturation in the revolutionary past" was initially outlined.[55] Although only two such cases of nationality expression were cited, this expression became more noticeable as the May riots faded further into the background.

The interaction between Party and Komsomol authorities and the educational institutions of the Lithuanian SSR should be viewed as only a part of an intricate weave of interactions occurring on a massive Union-wide scale. This interaction reflects upon only a single strand or aspect of Soviet nationality policy.

Although the Lithuanian SSR has not experienced an influx of large numbers of Russians as have other republics of the Soviet West, the Komsomol and Party leaderships (according to the press) are just as active in their efforts to publicize the need for cooperation on a Union-wide basis. The advanced economic level of some other republics of the Soviet West (the Ukraine, Latvia and Estonia) make these areas more appealing to Russians than is the case with Lithuania.

Moreover, Communist leaders in Latvia and Estonia are undertaking ideological campaigns "to foster ethnic tolerance and understanding" in the two republics.[56] As a result of the influx of outsiders,

there is now one Russian for every two Latvians in Latvia and one
Russian for every three Estonians in the Estonian SSR. However,
it must be noted that Roman Catholic Lithuania has maintained a ratio
of one Russian for every ten Lithuanians due to the Republic's
moderately high birth rate and low degree of out-migration.

Based on a detailed analysis of the evidence presented in this
study, one can conclude that ideological rejuvenation was clearly the
major preoccupation of Party and Komsomol authorities in the Lithuanian SSR. During the period under examination, the twin themes of
ideological preparation of cadres and involvement in the process of
modernization dominated the Russian-language press, providing
adequate reinforcement to the hypothesis that ideological campaigns
were viewed by the authorities as effective tools for redirecting or
minimizing nationality perseverance.

Ideological expertise, however, was coupled with efforts to
involve potential dissidents in the process of modernization, as the
Republic shifted from a basically agrarian-oriented economy to an
economy characterized by widespread development of light and heavy
industries. There was apparently a systematic effort to mold ideological and economic involvement into a viable and attractive alternative to religiously-based nationalism or the influences of Roman
Catholicism.

Though the evidence firmly supports the contention of this study,
it remains uncertain whether ideological activities or the promise
of greater economic participation are attracting Lithuanian youth in
sufficient measure to constitute effective channels into which nationality consciousness can be minimized.

NOTES

1. Chicago Tribune, August 8, 1971, p. 6. Report based on an
Associated Press dispatch from Moscow (August 7, 1971).
2. Ibid.
3. "A Lithuanian Samizdat Document," Radio Liberty Dispatch,
February 15, 1971, p. 1.
4. Theodore Shabad, "Lithuanians Cite Curb on Religion," New
York Times, September 27, 1971, p. 5. Also see Radio Liberty Dispatch, February 15, 1973, p. 9.
5. Chronicle of the Lithuanian Catholic Church, No. 2, (1972),
pp. 1-45.
6. Chronicle of the Lithuanian Catholic Church, No. 1, (1972).
Contained in the private papers of Professor A. Landsbergis of Fair-
leigh Dickinson University. These events also mentioned by Theodore
Shabad, New York Times, September 26, 1972, p. 15.

7. "The Persecution of Believers in Lithuania," Chronicle of Current Events, May 1972, Moscow, Issues 25 and 26, pp. 195-99.

8. Chronicle of Current Events, March 1971. Also see Radio Liberty Dispatch, February 15, 1973, p. 10.

9. Ibid.

10. Radio Liberty Dispatch, June 2, 1972, pp. 1-2.

11. Ibid., p. 2.

12. Theodore Shabad, "Lithuanian Trial of Eight Starts," New York Times, September 26, 1972, p. 15.

13. Radio Liberty Dispatch, June 2, 1972, p. 11.

14. Ibid.

15. ELTA Information Service, New York: Supreme Committee for the Liberation of Lithuania, October 1972, pp. 1-2.

16. "Druzhbu narodim slavim pesnei," Sovetskaia Litva, May 25, 1972, p. 1.

17. "Vesna, poezia, okrylennosti'," Sovetskaia Litva, May 27, 1972, p. 4.

18. "Recent Events Among Lithuanian Catholics," Radio Liberty Dispatch, February 15, 1973, p. 2.

19. Ibid.

20. Stephen P. Dunn, Cultural Processes in the Baltic Area Under Soviet Rule, (Berkeley: University of California, 1966), pp. 23-25.

21. "Uluchat' kommunisticheskoe vospitanie molodogi," Sovetskaia Litva, May 16, 1972, p. 2.

22. "Gostovit' vysokovalifitsirovannykh ideino-zrelykh spetsialistov," Sovetskaia Litva, October 20, 1972, pp. 1-2.

23. "Piatidesiatileties SSSR i zadachi ideologicheskoi raboty," Sovetskaia Litva, July 6, 1972, p. 1.

24. Ibid.

25. "Ob uchebe i vospitanie molodogi," Sovetskaia Litva, May 17, 1972, p. 1.

26. "Ekonomicheskaia ucheba kadrov," Sovetskaia Litva, June 3, 1972, p. 1.

27. V. Petin, "Shkola ideinoi zahkalki," Sovetskaia Litva, June 6, 1972, p. 2.

28. A. Lakniunene, "Nastoichivo ovladevat' teoriei," Sovetskaia Litva, June 16, 1972, p. 2.

29. "Povyshat' deistovennost' ideologicheskoi rabot'," Sovetskaia Litva, July 7, 1972, pp. 1-2.

30. Ibid., p. 2.

31. "Disiplina obiazatel'na dlia vsekh," Sovetskaia Litva, September 15, 1972, p. 2.

32. "Vospitanie na geroicheskikh traditsiakh, Sovetskaia Litva, September 24, 1972, p. 1.

33. "Ukreliati ideiniuu zakalkuu rukovodiashikh kadrov," Sovetskaia Litva, September 29, 1972, p. 1.

34. Ibid.

35. "Novii etap v zhizni Vuzov," Sovetskaia Litva, September 5, 1972, p. 2.

36. Mazoji Lietuvsko; Tarybue Encklopedia (Vilnius: Mintis, 1971), pp. 454-55.

37. "Vyschaia shkola i zadachi kommunisticheskgo stroitel' stva," Sovetskaia Litva, October 21, 1972, p. 2.

38. Ibid.

39. "V vechernem universitete," Sovetskaia Litva, September 28, 1972, p. 2.

40. A. Gedis, "Shkola osnov ekonomiki," Sovetskaia Litva, October 7, 1972, p. 1.

41. An Associated Press report published in the New York Times, June 14, 1971, pp. 1-5, fixed the ages of the arrested May demonstrators at 16 to 24 years.

42. "Vospityvat' patriotov," Sovetskaia Litva, March 30, 1972, p. 2.

43. "Zavershiuchshii etap ucheby," Sovetskaia Litva, April 12, 1972, p. 1.

44. N. Kobiuzev, "Plodi druzhbi i bratstva," Sovetskaia Litva, September 7, 1972, p. 2.

45. I. Manyushis, "The Fruits of Friendship," Soviet Life, November 1972, p. 15.

46. "Sem'ia, edinaia, druzhnaia," Sovetskaia Litva, July 14, 1972, p. 2.

47. "V sem'e edinoi," Sovetskaia Litva, July 7, 1972, p. 4.

48. "Naselenie nashei strany," Pravda, April 17, 1971, p. 2.

49. Ibid.

50. Antanas Sneckus, "Grazhdanin velikogo sovetskogo soiuza," Pravda, September 8, 1972, pp. 2-3.

51. Hederick Smith, "Lithuanian Saunas Draw Pravda Heat," New York Times, March 27, 1972, p. 16.

52. Sovetskaia Litva, September 12, 1972, p. 14.

53. "O predvaritel'nykh itogakh vsesoiuznoi perepisi naseleniia 1970 goda," Pravda, April 19, 1970, p. 2.

54. A. Barkauskas, "Istochniki vdokhnovenia," Komsomol'-skaia Pravda, January 18, 1972, p. 4.

55. "Forum khudozhnikov Litvy," Sovetskaia Litva, January 18, 1973, p. 4.

56. Theodore Shabad, "Migrants Worry Estonia, Latvia," New York Times, March 13, 1973, p. 4.

CHAPTER

8

FIFTY YEARS OF
SOVIET FEDERALISM
IN BELORUSSIA

Brian Connelly

    The evolution of Soviet nationality policy, the history of Soviet
federalism, and the fate of the Belorussian nationality are all intertwined in the Soviet slogans of "socialist in content, national in form"
and "the dialectic of the flourishing (rastsvet) and drawing together
(sblizhenie) of nations."* The first of these slogans, "socialist in
content, national in form," was initially advanced by Stalin in his
speech at the Communist University of Toilers of the East on May 18,
1925,[1] and, though it was intended as a characteristic of the culture
that the Communists were trying to foster, it serves as a useful
capsule description of Soviet federalism. As for the phrase, "the
flourishing and drawing together of nations," it means that at the
same time the nationalities are asserting their self-identity, they
are becoming more like all other nationalities of the federation.
The prominence of these formulations was reinforced during the
celebrations of 1972 in honor of the fiftieth anniversary of the formation of the Union of Soviet Socialist Republics, the federalist
vehicle for the "resolution" of the nationality question in the Soviet
Union.[2]
    In the opinion of some Western observers, this anniversary
also marked a renewed Soviet effort to homogenize its diverse nationalities. One journalist characterized the situation as follows:

> After 50 years of trying to knit its more than 100 ethnic
> groups into a single society, the Soviet Union appears to

---

    *Throughout this paper, reference is made to nation and na-
tionality interchangeably. To conform to common usage agreed upon
by all authors in this volume, nationality refers to a nation in the
Soviet meaning. In direct quotations, however, the word "nation" will
be retained.

have made great gains in the educational and cultural development of its nationalities. But it remains well short of the ultimate goal of total harmony. . . . [yet the] long-term tendency seems evident in the Soviet Union, aim[ing] ultimately at a vaguely defined integration of ethnic groups into a single Soviet nation.[3]

Prominent among those subjected to this integration effort are the nationalities of the Soviet West, the area of the USSR chosen as the focus of this collective study.

It is the hypothesis of this study that 50 years of Soviet federalism, with its concomitant "integrative" pressures (that is, social mobilization, educational leveling, modernization, and the like), has failed to alter substantially the nationality consciousness (the effective self-identity) of the Belorussian nationality. Furthermore, it is posited that the choice of a federal political structure for the USSR played an important role in the preservation of this self-identification while, at the same time, it promoted policies that led to changes in some of the more visible symbols of the Belorussian nationality. Therefore, an important aspect of the present study will be an examination of this dichotomy between the essence of a nationality and its attributes. The sociopolitical organization most intimately associated with this interaction between integrationist pressures (homogenization of attributes) and nationality consciousness (a resilient essence of nationality self-awareness) is the Communist party of the Soviet Union (CPSU), and we will examine its role (or, more precisely, the role of the Belorussian Communist party) in this process.

The choice of sources to document this struggle between integrative pressures and the vitality of the Belorussian nationality reflects the distinction made above between attributes and essence. The examination of the effect of integrative pressures upon the attributes of the Belorussian nationality draws heavily upon data from the 1959 and 1970 Soviet censuses and Soviet statistical yearbooks,[4] with periodic reference to the local press for corroboration. However, research into the question of the all-important essence of the Belorussian nationality depended especially on evidence from two daily Russian-language newspapers published in the Belorussian SSR: Sovetskaia Belorussiia, the organ of the Communist party of the BSSR (surveyed from September 1972 through January 1973, with a sampling of issues taken from earlier in 1972), and Znamia iunosti, the Republic's Komsomol paper (surveyed for November and December 1972).

This chapter has six sections: (1) a brief treatment of the terminology and definitions that are essential to the study; (2) a sketch of the context (within the federal political structure, within an identifiable regional grouping called the "Soviet West," and within the BSSR) of the struggle between integrative pressures and nationality consciousness; (3) a description of the organizations (the Party and Komsomol) interacting with the general public, especially the Russian-speaking segment, in this scenario; (4) an analysis of the effect of integrative pressures on the attributes of the Belorussian nationality; (5) an analysis of the effect of integrative pressures on the essence of the Belorussian nationality; and (6) concluding remarks concerning the weight to be attached to each factor in the struggle for nationality perseverance and the probable applicability of the Belorussian example to the study of nationality perseverance in the Soviet West and in the USSR in general.

TERMINOLOGY AND DEFINITIONS

Background for this investigation of the nationality question in the Belorussian Soviet Socialist Republic (BSSR) included a survey of some of the recent Western literature dealing with the concepts of nationalism (especially with regard to multinational states) and integration (particularly as applied to the European Economic Community).[5] From the former, distinctions between the terms "national" and "state" were culled, while from the latter some useful subdivisions of the concept of integration were derived.

This evaluation of the past half-century of Soviet federalism depends heavily on the correct usage of the terms "nationality" and "state." For the purposes of this study, a "nationality" will be defined as "a social group which shares a common ideology, common institutions and customs, and essense of homogeneity," and a state as "a legal concept describing a social group that occupies a defined territory and is organized under common political institutions and an effective government."[6] In addition to these definitions, however, it is also necessary to be conversant with two Soviet variants: the standard definition by Stalin and one of the latest attempts to update it. For Stalin, a nation (that is, what we are calling a nationality) was "an historically evolved, stable community of people, formed on the basis of a common language, territory, economic life, and psychological makeup manifested in a common culture."[7] In refining some of Stalin's criteria, a debate in the pages of the Soviet journal Volprosy istorii produced the following updated version:

> A nation is an historically evolved community of indi-
> viduals, characterized by stable community of eco-
> nomic life (with the existence of a working class),
> territory, language (especially a literary language),

and self-consciousness of ethnic identity, as well as by
some specific features of psychology and traditions of
everyday life, culture and struggle for liberation.[8]

The inclusion of the concept of "self-conscious ethnic identity" in the
second definition will be of considerable importance in this analysis
of the struggle between integrationist pressures and nationality endurance in Belorussia.

A further distinction that is necessary for a proper understanding
of this study's hypothesis is the difference between the attributes of
a nationality and its essence. Because the concept of a nationality
is a difficult abstraction to grasp, there is a tendency to seize upon
its tangible characteristics (for example, numbers, religious composition, language, geographic location, and the like) and identify the
nationality with these concrete factors.[9] Often the members of a
nationality will elevate such a visible attribute of their group to the
status of a symbol.[10] However, these characteristics of a nationality
are significant only to the extent to which they contribute to the group's
self-identity and uniqueness, and a nationality can lose or alter all
of these attributes without losing the sense of vital uniqueness which
makes it a nationality.[11] Therefore, the essence of a nationality is
intangible, "a psychological bond that joins a people and differentiates
it, in the subconscious conviction of its members, from all other people
in a most vital way,"[12]

The two elements at work in the struggle between integrationist
pressures and nationality consciousness are "assimilation" and "national self-determination," respectively. The former can be defined
as "the adoption of the culture of another social group to such an
extent that the person or group no longer has any characteristics
identifying him with his former culture and no longer has any particular loyalties to his former culture."[13] The latter can be defined
as a nation's "right to choose freely [its] political, economic and
social systems, including the right to establish an independent national state, to pursue [its] development and dispose of [its] natural
wealth and resources."[14] The dual tendencies of the flourishing
and drawing together of nationalities are the dialectical expressions
given by Soviet ideologists to this struggle. Though they would undoubtedly hedge at characterizing the "flourishing" of nationalities
as representative of the force of nationality self-determination at
work (a drive whose power they respect and fear), such theorists
would probably be less hesitant to agree that the "drawing together"
depicts the assimilationist/integrationist tendencies.

THE CONTEXT OF INTERACTION BETWEEN
INTEGRATION AND NATIONALITY CONSCIOUSNESS

With these definitions as guideposts, the next step in this investigation is a brief treatment of the context in which the interaction
between integrative pressures and nationality consciousness takes
place. The overall framework is the Soviet federal system, which
provides both the "arena" and the "rules of the game," for this interaction. The choice of a federal structure for the Soviet Union was
a very deliberate one, and the only logical one in the opinion of many
authorities on Soviet history.[15] Despite the economic benefits to be
derived from a unitary state, it is reasonable to conclude that Lenin
viewed the federal structure as a vehicle for solving the nationality
question. Thus, the form of the Soviet state appears to have been
designed precisely to handle the interaction between integrative pressures (associated with sblizhenie) and nationality consciousness (associated with rastsvet). Soviet federalism can therefore be viewed
as a hybrid of socialist goals and as a nationality vehicle, embodying
the slogan of "socialist in content, national in form."[16]

Reviewing the many traits that the republics of the Soviet West
have in common and seeing that they have been subjected to similar
integrative pressures, strongly emphasizes the one notable exception
to their similarities, that is, the weak native tradition of Belorussia.
This makes Belorussia an especially interesting arena for the struggle
between integrative pressures and nationality endurance.

Historically, Belorussians, as Eastern Slavs, can trace common
ties with the Ukrainians and Russians back to the kingdom of Kievan
Rus'.[17] When the Mongol invasion of the thirteenth century caused
the division of Kievan Rus' into three areas (West Russia—Belorussia;
South Russia—the Ukraine; and Northeast Russia—Russia), the western
principalities (the area that was to become Belorussia) sought pro-
tection from Lithuania. The combined Lithuano-Belorussian state
was known as the Grand Duchy of Lithuania. Belorussian scholars
point with pride to the fact that the administrative language of this
medieval empire, which extended from the Baltic to the Black Sea,
was Belorussian. However, this Belorussian influence was eventually
supplanted by Polish predominance as Poland and Lithuania were
joined in 1386, and merged in 1569. The bulk of the Belorussian
nationality (that is, the peasantry) was relatively unaffected by this
process of Polonization, but then peasants rarely identified with any
grouping larger than their village.

The three partitions of Poland between 1772 and 1795 restored
Belorussia to Russian rule, but the Czars were no more eager to
foster a Belorussian identity than the Poles had been. In fact, Belorussia was renamed the Northwestern Territory and Nicholas I, by

a decree of July 18, 1840, forbade the use of the term "Belorussia."[18] Though there were intellectuals who kept the concept of a Belorussian identity alive, it took the 1917 Russian revolution to give it a chance to blossom. There was an ill-fated independent Belorussian National Republic proclaimed while Belorussia was under German occupation (March 25, 1918 to December 9, 1918), but it was overthrown with the return of Bolshevik forces. It was not until January 1, 1919, that an effective state structure, the Belorussian Soviet Socialist Republic, was founded for Belorussia. It is within this context that the inter- action between integrationist pressures and nationality consciousness will be examined, for it has been pointed out that "the very existence, for the first time in history, of a formal republic called Belorussia, has served as a focal point for the development of a national identity during the last 50 years."[19]

SOCIAL ORGANIZATION AND INTERACTION

The interplay between integrative pressures and nationality endurance involves social organizations and individuals. In view of the Communist party's self-proclaimed role as the leading element of Soviet society, it would be both difficult and unwise to overlook the Party's involvement in the question of integrative pressures and nationality consciousness. The guiding role of the Party is asserted constantly in the press, where it is noted that "communist society, in contrast to all preceding social structures, does not form spon- taneously but as the result of the conscious, purposeful activities of the masses, guided by the Marxist-Leninist party [emphasis added]."[20] P. M. Masherov, First Secretary of the Belorussian Communist party, observed that "the Belorussian people, like all the peoples of our country, are infinitely grateful to their indigenous Communist party."[21]

It is interesting that this indigenous Communist party (the BCP) which supposedly shapes and molds society in Belorussia also reflects its ethnic diversity. According to the latest available figures (January 1, 1968) the breakdown of the BCP is roughly as follows: (1) total membership—379,221; (2) Belorussians—265,400 [70 percent]; (3) Russians—70,142 [18.5 percent]; (4) Ukrainians—16,576 [4.4 per- cent]; and (5) other nationalities—27,103 [7.1 percent].[22] The Rus- sians are apparently overrepresented in the ranks of the BCP because they comprise 18.5 percent of the BCP though they account for only 10.4 percent of the population of the BSSR.[23] This, however, can be explained by the tendency of the Party to draw its membership more heavily from the urban population of any given republic, coupled with statistics showing that the Russians make up 19.6 percent of the urban population of the BSSR.[24] Finally, the leadership of the

BCP is clearly Belorussian—the First Secretary of the BCP, P. M. Masherov, is Belorussian, as are eight of the 12 members of the BCP's Bureau (of the remaining four, one is Russian and three are of undetermined ethnicity).[25] Therefore, as this investigation turns to an examination of the Party's role in the integrative process, it should be kept in mind that the effects of this process are working not only upon the ethnic composition of Soviet society, in general, and Belorussian society, in particular, but also upon the ethnic composition of the CPSU, in general, and the BCP, in particular.

The Party's actual role in the interaction between integrative pressures and nationality consciousness falls into the category of promoting integration, though often subtly. Historically, its role is described as follows:

> In the establishment of the friendship of peoples, as in all our achievements, a decisive role was played by the Communist party of the Soviet Union. Directing a real internationalist course in the sphere of national relations, the Party protects and strengthens this friendship in every possible way as one of the basic achievements of socialism. On all levels of Communist construction, the Party led the decisive struggle against any nationalistic manifestations or remnants.[26]

The phrase "friendship of people" (druzhba narodov) would seem to suggest at least a tolerance for nationality distinctions, but nationalistic manifestations were to be rooted out at the same time. Therefore, it might be concluded that to be different was permissible as long as attention was not called to the difference.

Current Party policy, is, as noted earlier, governed by the dialectic of the flourishing and the drawing together of nationalities. Though the origin of the phrase itself is uncertain, it achieved prominence at the XXII Congress of the CPSU in October 1961, when Khrushchev proclaimed: "each nation is undergoing a tempestuous all-around development and the rights of the Union and Autonomous republics are expanding . . . [while] under the banner of proletarian internationalism the socialist nations are drawing ever closer together."[27] Though the Party is pledged to support both tendencies, its predilection for the integrationist policy of "drawing together" can be seen in Brezhnev's speech at the ceremonies commemorating the fiftieth anniversary:

> The further drawing together of the nations and nationalities of our country is an objective process. [emphasis added] The Party is against pushing the process;

this is needless, for it is determined by the entire course of our Soviet life. At the same time, the Party considers as impermissible any attempt to hold it up, to impede it on some pretext, or artificially to consolidate national distinctiveness, [emphasis added] because this would go against the general line of development of our society, the internationalist ideals and the ideology of Communists, the interests of Communist construction.[28]

This presents, quite clearly, the thrust of current Party policy on the nationality question. Despite a disclaimer that it is unnecessary to "push" the drawing together of nationalities, it is clear that the efforts of the Party will be directed toward promoting, however subtly, the drawing together of nationalities.

The other group with a potential to foster an affirmative image of the drawing together of nationalities is the Komsomol. Secretary Brezhnev gave a fairly accurate capsule description of the role of the Komsomol when, in describing the desired characteristics of a Komsomol activist, he said: "Life continuously raises demands for cadres [and we] need people, combining high political consciousness with good professional preparation [emphasis added]."[29] Therefore, the Komsomol is also seen to act as a conduit for the ideas of the Party into the various professions and trades of Soviet society.

Because of the position that the Party and Komsomol occupy in Soviet society, their combined influence is apparently all-pervasive. Members of the Party or Komsomol generally occupy the key positions in any significant aspect of Soviet society. Thus, a Party decision to promote integrative pressures would be reflected in industry, government, education, and other fields, as individual Party and Komsomol members worked to bring their organization into line. However, the Party takes great care not to offend nationality sensibilities, so a certain concern is shown to portray their efforts as an attempt to foster a supranational identity (a Soviet identity) rather than as an attempt to "denationalize" any group.

One of the key elements in any such campaign is the press. Since it is essentially the self-identification of the people that the Party is trying to manipulate, it is important to shape the image that the members of a nationality have of themselves. In addition to attempts to portray favorably those events that reflect the desired trend (that is, the drawing together of nationalities), it is useful to analyze the coverage given to the opposite trend (that is, the flourishing of a nationality). Identifying activities that seem to indicate a certain degree of nationality consciousness take on an added significance because they would have to satisfy the stipulation mentioned in Secretary Brezhnev's speech, that they represent the interest in the nationality (in this case, the Belorussian nationality) without artificially consolidating nationality distinctiveness. This is a very fine line to tread.

ATTRIBUTES OF THE BELORUSSIAN NATIONALITY

Keeping in mind the definitional distinctions delineated earlier in this study, the investigation now turns to an examination of integrative pressures brought to bear upon the attributes of the Belorussian nationality.

One of the factors that make the study of the Belorussian nationality of particular importance to those concerned with the overall nationality question in the Soviet Union is the often-voiced doubt about both the Belorussian nationality's right to exist and its chances for continued survival. The historical doubt came to light in a speech by Stalin to the X Congress of the RCP(b) on March 10, 1921, in which he said:

> I have received a note alleging that we Communists are
> artificially cultivating a Byelorussian nationality. That
> is not true, for there exists a Byelorussian nation, which
> has its own language, different from Russian. Conse-
> quently, the culture of the Byelorussian people can be
> raised only in its native language.[30]

The contemporary doubt was expressed by the Belorussian emigré scholar Nicholas Vakar, who noted in 1968 that "[t]he view that the Belorussian people is an established nation has been losing ground lately; the view that it is a national minority doomed to extinction in our time has gained ascendency."[31]

Prompting the recent pessimism are the 1970 Soviet census figures that record that the Belorussians, among the titular nationalities of the Soviet West, had the lowest percentage (80.6 percent) of people regarding their nationality language as their native tongue and the highest proportion of those indicating a fluency in Russian (49 percent) or another Soviet language (7.3 percent).[32] Though, as was pointed out earlier, language is only an attribute of a nationality's self-identity and not its essence, language is generally regarded as an important symbol of the nationality's strength. Therefore, any loss in the proportion of the given nationality indicating use of their nationality tongue as their primary language is usually viewed as an indicator of possible, even probable, assimilation of that nationality into the nationality whose language is gaining adherents. Thus, one of the integrative pressures that must be considered is the encouragement by the Party of a command of the Russian language by Belorussians.

114

However, a further analysis of the above-mentioned data is needed, because they include all Belorussians, both inside and out of the BSSR. It is those Belorussians living outside of the BSSR that present the most likely target of assimilation (both linguistic and otherwise). This is confirmed by reference to additional data from the 1970 census indicating that 90.1 percent of the Belorussians living within the BSSR consider Belorussian their primary language, whereas only 40.8 percent of the Belorussians living outside the Republic feel likewise.[33] In commenting on a similar set of figures from the 1959 census, a Soviet scholar observed:

> Finding themselves among the native population of other republics having strongly pronounced specific, everyday, social, economic, cultural, linguistic, and other features, Belorussians, the same as any other national minority in the given republic, will feel an especially strong Russian influence in language and all other relations . . . concerning the strength of those processes, these facts may testify. In the Belorussian SSR, 93.2 percent of the Belorussians consider the language of their nationality to be their native tongue. Among those finding themselves beyond the borders of their republic, only 30 percent of Belorussians consider Belorussian as their native language.[34]

Thus, the Belorussians outside of their titular republic have exhibited a natural tendency to adapt to their minority status within the republic in which they reside. In general, they find themselves without schools to teach Belorussian and forced either to opt for the local language or Russian, which is the primary inter-nationality contact language (iazyk mezhnatsional'nogo obshcheniia).

The Russian-speaking Belorussians within the BSSR, particularly those who identify Russian as their primary language, are of particular interest for this study. Though the Irish, among others, have demonstrated that a nationality can maintain a strong self-identity even after it loses its own language as its primary means of communication, the current battle between Belorussian and linguistically assimilationist inroads of Russian remains significant.

The use of the Russian language in schools and universities in Belorussia, and the dominance of Russian in book, journal, and newspaper publishing, naturally contributes to linguistic russification. The use of Russian as a native language by Belorussians is most pronounced among young, school and college age people. Thus, in an effort to promote integrationist pressures—the drawing together of nationalities—the Party endorses the study of Russian, but official caution and concern for nationality sensibilities frames this support in terms of a knowledge of Russian in addition to the nationality language. The two chief areas of language conflict in the struggle between integrationist pressures and nationality consciousness appear to be education and publishing.

But, as with all dialectical processes, the linguistic drawing together of nations in Belorussia has been offset, to a certain extent, by a parallel flourishing of the Belorussian language through an increase in the absolute numbers speaking Belorussian and the absolute number of works printed in Belorussian. Furthermore, there are even some indications of a limited counter-pressure, offered, for instance, by speakers at the Sixth Congress of the Union of Belorussian Writers, in April 1971, demanding that the publication of books in Belorussia reflect census figures showing that better than 80 percent of all Belorussians consider Belorussian as their native tongue.[35]

In evaluating the role of the Party in promoting the use of Russian, the particular care traditionally shown by the Party for not only the kinds of ideas promulgated in the Soviet Union but also the method of dissemination must be kept in mind. In addition to the overt support of the Russian language given in the Party program, tacit support is given to Russian linguistic assimilation when the Party, as guardian of the educational system and author of the master plan allocating newsprint and other raw materials for printing, condones (if not actually promotes) the Russification of higher education and the imbalance in favor of Russian-language publications in the BSSR. A further indication of the impact of Russian linguistic penetration is the fact that Kommunist Belorussii, the ideological journal of the Belorussian Communist party, is published only in Russian (the Belorussian edition, Kamunist Belarusi, was closed down in 1962).[36] This situation would seem to denote at least an indirect acknowledgement that Russian is the language of ideas in the BSSR.

Given the Party's apparent support of the linguistic inroads of Russian in the BSSR and evidence of distinct encroachment of Russian in the fields of education and publishing, some appraisal of the "threat" of linguistic assimilation for the Belorussian nationality must be offered. Census figures show that the Belorussians exhibit the lowest level of identification with their native tongue of any of the titular union republic nationality in the Soviet West or USSR, but Belorussians (within their republic) still identify with their own language by an overwhelming majority. This is a key point, for it demonstrates that the existence of a Belorussian republic (territorial attribute) as an integral part of Soviet federalism has acted to reinforce the language identification of the Belorussian nationality by providing it with a homeland as a supportive mechanism.[37]

Perhaps the most striking impact of federalism has concerned the territorial attribute of the Belorussian nationality. The formation of the Soviet Union, in effect, sanctioned the creation of a Belorussian state, the first (discounting the German puppet state of the months immediately after the Brest Treaty of March 1918) really viable political expression of the Belorussian nationality. There are those who will object that there can be no Belorussian state because a state must be sovereign and Belorussia's "sovereignty," evidenced by its membership in the UN, is extremely limited. However, one Western scholar has offered the following rejoinder to this type of objection:

> But if sovereignty is one of the four necessary character-istics of a state, how does one account for the fact that the sovereignty of some states is merely a fiction and that it varies greatly among the remainder? It is evident that sovereignty is not in actuality a prerequisite of state-hood [emphasis added]. Because of the political and ana-lytical problems associated with measuring such an ab-straction [i.e., sovereignty], state governments have in practice developed and honored a myth that all states are equally and fully possessed of sovereignty. If a unit has territory, population, and government; if that govern-ment desires the unit to be recognized as a state; and if the governments of other states wish to so recognize it, then sovereignty is imputed regardless of the actual situation.[38]

In addition to this Soviet-sponsored sovereignty, the Belorussian Republic also benefited from adjustments of its borders. This began with cessions of territory to the BSSR by the RSFSR (including parts of the Vitebsk and Gomel oblasts) and the Ukraine in 1923 and 1924, and from the post-World War II settlement, the Belorussians emerged with a territory approximately 60 percent larger, at the expense of Poland.[39]

It is difficult to overestimate the importance of federalism to the territorial attribute of the Belorussian nationality. Certainly the form of Belorussian territory owes everything to federalism, but the BSSR's classification as a union republic and its carefully cultivated "sovereignty" as a member of the UN add another important dimension to its identity. The fact that these symbols could be re-moved without crippling the Belorussian identity does not mean that they have had no effect on the sense of ethnic self-identity as highly visible symbols of Belorussianness.

In order to control its federal creation the Party long ago decided to prevent a federalization of its own ranks.[40] It took great pains to see that the "national form" of republics such as the BSSR did not affect the "socialist content" of their titular nationalities. Since the reality of living in their own homeland serves to reinforce the self-identity of the Belorussians, the Party is obliged to counter the possibility of excessive national distinctiveness by reminding Belorussians of their concurrent identity as part of the Soviet people.

The economic development of Belorussia is another attribute of Belorussian nationality which has been influenced by the Soviet state. Lenin laid down the priority of developing the economically backward Soviet republics, such as Belorussia, and great strides toward that goal have been made. Since 1913, the total volume of industrial production in Belorussia increased by 113 percent, and the economy of the Republic is shifting from agriculture to manufacturing.[41]

Just as the Party is wary lest the existence of a Belorussian nationality territory fosters an excessive sense of ethnic distinctiveness, so too it seeks to temper a sense of nationality pride in the economic accomplishments of the BSSR by constantly pointing out that these gains occurred within the context of the Soviet federation. For example, one report in 1972 speculated: "Would Belorussia's workers have been able to establish such gigantic industries as the tractor and automobile factory in Minsk with their own hands alone? Of course not!"[42] The message is clear; the BSSR would not have made it to where it is today without the help of its fellow republics.

However, the effects of this interdependence are not seen as exclusively economic. A presumed by-product of this interaction is a reinforcement of the feeling of unity among the various nationalities. This theme also received coverage in the press:

> This fraternal exchange of products, technical achievements and advanced experience helps personnel in many enterprises of Belorussia and Moscow to move forward confidently along the path of technical progress and the perfection of production, and it strengthens the friendship of the Belorussian and Russian peoples as members of the united family of peoples of the great Soviet Union.[43]

Underlying this idea of the "strengthening of the friendship" between nationalities and Russians is an integrationist bias evident at least since Lenin observed: "Economics really . . . is a force merging nations."[44]

This presumption that economic integration will have a "spillover" effect and foster some kind of assimilation is not unique to Lenin and the Soviet Union. It enjoyed a brief popularity, for example, among idealists in the West who hoped that the economic integration of the European Economic Commity would lead not only to a form of political integration but also to a genuine pan-European identity, concurrent with or possibly supplanting the various national identities. Today, however, while many still believe in the inevitability of political integration from economic "spillover," only a few diehards still cling to the idea of a pan-European identity, even as a long-term possibility.

Though the Soviet Union, in effect, achieved economic and political integration at the same time with the creation of the USSR (in 1922), the successful fostering of a Soviet identity remains a debatable point. In fact, it can be argued that, in large part due to the federalist form of political integration chosen as the societal framework, economic integration has produced a sense of "relative deprivation"[45] among the Belorussians rather than promoting any supranational identity, either as elements of the Soviet people or residents of the Soviet West.

It is the federal structure of the Soviet Union that really serves to highlight the sense of relative deprivation, though federalism was among other things intended to correct economic imbalances among the nationalities of the USSR and has, in fact, achieved absolute increases in the economic welfare of the various nationalities, For example, the newspapers report that, in just the past few years, the BSSR has witnessed the construction of chemical plants in Novopolotsk, Grodno, Mogilev, Gomel, Soligorsk and Svetlogorsk, the opening of electronics factories in Minsk, Vitebsk, and Brest, and the development of light industry in Baranovich, Pinsk, and Orsh.[46] Yet, despite these absolute gains, the economy of the BSSR is still the second weakest, after Moldavia, in the Soviet West.[47]

Though Brezhnev may claim that "the task of equalizing the economic development of the various republics has, by and large, been completed,"[48] it is clear to any Belorussian who looks at the figures published in Soviet sources that his nationality's territory lags behind, for example, the territory of his Estonian fellow inhabitant of the Soviet West. This sense of relative deprivation would clearly act to undercut any feeling of common Soviet Western identity since it would reaffirm the "us-them" dichotomy. Compounding the problem of relative backwardness in comparison to their (Soviet) Western neighbors is the insecurity of the Belorussians vis-à-vis the Russians residing in Belorussia. Though the federal structure of the USSR promotes a feeling that a nationality should be master of its own house (its nationality territory), the Belorussians like many other titular nationalities find themselves unsure in that role due to the special position of the Russians in the BSSR. To cite only one example, the Russians are represented out of proportion to their numbers in the total of specialists with higher education in Belorussia.[49]

In this confusion of absolute versus relative gains by the Belorussian economy, the Party's role is to emphasize the absolute gains and ignore, wherever possible, examples of relative inequality. In seeking a self-description of the Party's importance with regard to the economic gains made by the Belorussians, an observation made concerning a particular Party unit in a factory can be borrowed and endowed with a broader application:

> These successes became possible because the Party organization—all its members—ensured, always together with the workers and the public, progressive movement forward through their accomplishments, skill, and organization.[50]

However, the Party's efforts to focus attention on Belorussia's current economic position, solely in comparison with its pre-Soviet level of development run afoul of the human tendency to measure one's success in terms of the comparative status of those around oneself at the moment. Therefore, how far a nationality has come is rarely as important as its perception of how far it still has to go. Furthermore, since self-identity depends heavily upon perceptions of "us-them" relationships, any reinforcement of the identification of "them" has a similar effect on the sense of "us." On the whole, therefore, the attributes of the Belorussian nationality have fared rather well and continue to reinforce sense of self-identity.

THE ESSENCE OF BELORUSSIAN NATIONALITY

This sense of self-identity is the essence of the Belorussian nationality, and it is beneficial to keep in mind the observation of one American political scientist that "the prime cause of political disunity is the absence of a single psychological focus shared by all segments of the population."[51] Soviet leaders, especially Party leaders, are well aware of this political maxim and after roughly fifty years of social engineering they announced at the XXIV CPSU Congress in 1971 that

> as a result of the development and drawing together of socialist classes and nations in the process of building socialism and communism in our country 'a new historical community of people—the Soviet people [narod] came into existence.'[52]

The kind of psychological focus that the Soviet leadership is offering in the concept of the Soviet people has an interesting duality to it, displayed in one of the definitions of "Soviet people" put forward in the Belorussian press at the end of 1972:

> It [that is, the narod] appears, in the first place, as a class community [emphasis added] uniting all the classes and social groups of socialist society and, in the second place, as an international community uniting the more than 100 nations, nationalities, and national groups populating the USSR.[53]

Thus, this identity combined economic and ethnic elements. This duality is supported by the decision to refer to a Soviet narod rather than a Soviet natsiia. The former term (narod) joins the concept of ethnicity (since it can be translated as "nation") with the idea of class (because an alternative definition is "the laboring population of a country").[54]

Though the following interpretation of the reasons for the Soviet leaders' choice of the term "narod" may be open to challenge, it seems that this reading is well-founded. The use of the phrase "historical community of people" in the proclamation of the XXIV Party Congress describing the narod is of special significance because this formulation is also used in the definitions of both natsiia (nation) and narodnost' (nationality), terms which represent clear ethnic self-identification.[55] Referring to the Soviet narod as the "historical community" would therefore seem to indicate a desire on the part of Soviet leaders to establish at least the para-ethnic claims of the Soviet "people" to the loyalty of all the inhabitants of the USSR. Yet, the class-unification aspect of the Soviet people also makes it obvious that the Party intended to imbue the concept of the Soviet people with a certain sense of supraethnicity, one that, in effect, substituted an economic bond—membership in the class of those working for the building of communism—for the cultural-historical ties of ethnicity.

Another aspect of promoting the concept of a nation (a self-aware ethnic group) not usually referred to by Soviet authors is the idea of political integration that involves a presumed shift in a person's focus of loyalty. This alteration or molding of a new nationality identity is generally seen as the end result of a process of modernization. Among the acknowledged indicators of modernization are the following: (1) urbanization, (2) geographic mobility, (3) achievement of the minimum (incomplete secondary) level of education necessary for skilled labor roles, and (4) attainment of higher education and specialized training.[56]

In analyzing these indicators in the Belorussian context, it is clear that, for example, the process of urbanization still has a long way to go in the Belorussian Republic. The 1972 figures reveal that only 46 percent of the Belorussian nationality in the BSSR is urbanized. This proportion, however, is up from 43 percent in 1970 and only 14 percent in 1913, within the current borders of the BSSR.[57] Though their index of localization is fairly high—80.5 percent of the Belorussians live in their nationality republic[58]—the Belorussians have demonstrated a function in Central Asia, and perhaps even in the Baltic republics, as disseminators of either Russification or the virtues of Slavdom.[59] In 1972, for example, over 100,000 young Belorussians were participating in the construction of electrical energy stations, factories, and other such projects in Siberia, the Soviet Far East, and the Far North of the Russian Republic.[60] In educational achievements, the Belorussians have fared relatively well. Between 1959 and 1970 the number of Belorussians with an incomplete secondary education (the minimum for skilled labor) per 1000 of the general population rose from 185 to 215, which compared favorably with the statistics for other Soviet Western nationalities.[61] Similarly, their proportions in higher and specialized education experienced an increase.[62] Thus, the Belorussians score effectively with regard to each indicator, allowing an assumption that modernization has taken place and continues to take place in Belorussia. What is not clear is which (if either) identity—Soviet or Belorussian—is being enhanced by this process of modernization.

The presumption among some Western scholars, until recently, has been that such modernization led inevitably to a leveling of all competing internal forms of ethnic self-identification within a country and the formation of a common nationality self-identity coterminous with the state. The ability of different ethnic groups to work together for modernization has generally been interpreted as a sign of a newly-forged and shared nationality identity. However, this viewpoint has now been called into question. It has been pointed out that

> [e]thnic consciousness is not an automatic bar to cooperative, nor even to coordinated or integrated, activities against a mutually perceived enemy or in pursuit of a mutually desired goal [that is, modernization]. A number of ethnic groups can, and often do, march under the same banner and shout the same slogans. All too often, however, such a composite movement has been misidentified as a manifestation of a single, all-embracing nationalism [emphasis added].[63]

The veracity of this caveat is easily proved, for example, by reference to any one of the multinational states of the Third World that emerged from the struggle against colonialism as apparent models of cohesion, only to fall apart in ensuing years as the loss of an external "them" led to a resurgence of internal "us-them" perceptions, based on traditional ethnic ties.

While social engineers in many of these countries have frantically sought to substitute a common goal, such as building a native socialist system like the idea of ujamaa in Nyrere's Tanzania, for the old external enemy, they have, at best, muted rather than eliminated the internal ethnic rivalries in their countries.

Soviet leaders, like their counterparts in the world's other multinational states, have opted for the use of a common goal (in this case, "building Communism") to smooth over potential ethnic rivalries. Furthermore, they possess a deep-seated faith in the ability of the process of building Communism to alter the make-up of the participants—the nationalities of the USSR—chiefly through the nationalities' constant interaction with one another. It is assumed, probably incorrectly, by Soviet leaders that this interaction will reinforce the perception of what these nationalities have in common (leading to the concept of the Soviet people), rather than what differentiates them—their ethnic self-identities. It has been perceptively noted that

> [though] more intensive contacts among parts of a population that has some foundation for a sense of common origin [emphasis added] will increase that consciousness . . . with groups whose customs and beliefs bespeak, on balance, not a common history but distinctive origins and development [emphasis added], increased contacts tend to have the opposite effect. Rather than strengthening the appeal of those traits held in common, there is a tendency to emphasize the traits which divide [emphasis added]. The great increase in tensions which a multitude of multiethnic states have been experiencing underlines this dichotomy.[64]

It appears that the concept of the Soviet people, rooted in a sense of common origin based on the "proletarian revolution of 1917," cannot override the concept of the Belorussian nationality (despite its apparent weaknesses), rooted in a sense of common origin based on an ethnic tradition dating back to Kievan Rus'.

Soviet scholars, too, are beginning to recognize the persistence of the "flourishing" aspect of the nationality dialectic, despite increased contacts:

a dialectical contradiction is found here in that such contacts, which are developing not only in the ethnic borderlands but also in the hearts of ethnic territories, and which are creating the basis for an exchange of elements of culture and ultimately for developing the process of drawing together, at times are accompanied by a strengthening of attention to national self-determination, by intensification of national self-consciousness.[65]

Given this acknowledgment of the continued existence of nationality self-consciousness, it remains to examine this phenomenon in the Belorussian case. It is worthwhile also to review some of the restrictions that circumscribe an outsider's investigation of the essence of the Belorussian nationality (its ethnic self-identity). First, the controlled press, serving as a primary source, will hardly print a blatant expression of nationality consciousness along the lines of "better a Belorussia run like hell by Belorussians than a Belorussia run like heaven by Moscow." Should some brave soul utter such a phrase, its chances of appearing in the pages of Sovetskaia Belorusiia or Znamia iunosti are nil. Second, any expressions of nationality self-awareness that are found in the press, though Belorussian enough to be vital, will probably have to be mild enough not to offend the Russian inhabitants of the BSSR who comprise the primary audience of the press we are scanning. Finally, what is discovered should have extra significance attributed to it because, in order to be passed by the censors, it presumably had to satisfy Brezhnev's dictum on not "artificially" consolidating nationality distinctiveness.

Because so much emphasis has been placed upon the ideas of cooperation and "mutual enrichment" of nationalities by the Soviet leaders, the Belorussian contribution to these interactions would seem a natural place to search for some evidence of nationlity endurance in view of the above-stated belief that such contacts reinforce nationality self-identity. Moreover, in surveying the examples of cooperation and "mutual enrichment" cited in the Russian-language press of the BSSR, another variety of the use of the ambiguous term narod arises. This time narod refers to the the Belorussian nationality and again it seems that the choice of terminology was deliberate. Utilization of this term, for example, in articles describing the Belorussian input into the system of cooperation, especially economic cooperation, allows not only a feeling of nationality pride on the part of ethnic Belorussians but also a feeling of civic pride on the part of members of other nationalities who call Belorussia home.

Illustrations of this dual pride are varied. In one report it was stated that "[a]t this time in our country [the USSR] there is no region where the products of Belorussia are not received."[66] Another announced that "[t]he machines of the Ordzhonikidze factory in Minsk are used in half of all the automated control systems of the national economy of the USSR."[67] In addition to these inputs into the Union-wide economy, the Belorussians, both indigenous and other citizens of the BSSR, take pride in the accomplishments of their scientists. These achievements range from the rather esoteric discovery of "the effect of irregular increases of speed and height on the rising of liquids in capillaries under the influence of ultrasonics"[68] by a member of the Belorussian Academy of Sciences, to the more immediately practical development by a team of Belorussian scientists of new "rotary methods for processing metal" (which, when applied in a Moscow factory, increased productivity four-fold).[69] Finally, there was even a note of ethnic/civic pride in a report about the Belorussian members (especially the gymnast Olga Korbut) of the Soviet Olympic team: "The envoys of Belorussian sports contributed 11 gold, 6 silver, and 2 bronze medals to the [total] received by Soviet sportsmen [at the Olympics]."[70] Had Belorussia been entered on its own, this would have qualified it for sixth place in total medals at the 1972 Olympics.[71]

Though tractors and computers made in the BSSR are a source of pride to the Belorussian nationality and help reinforce its self-identity to the extent that they represent concrete examples of Belorussian know-how, they do not really provide the insight into the essence of the Belorussian nationality that is vital to this study. Belorussian music and art have certainly had an effect on Belorussian self-identity for, as one article pointed out, "[i]n the figurative language of art, the artists of Belorussia [have] told the stern and beautiful history of the life of our homeland."[72] However, the two towering figures of Belorussian nationality culture were authors (Yanka Kupala and Yakub Kolas), so the treatment, in the Belorussian press, of the literary aspect of Belorussian nationality consciousness will be examined to provide the desired insight. Without attempting to offer any meaningful critique of the work of these two men, it is worthwhile to note that their literary virtues are extolled by Belorussian emigrant scholars[73] as well as the Soviet Belorussian press.

The importance of Kupala and Kolas to Belorussian literature is made very clear, even in the Russian-language press, where they are acknowledged as the "founders of a new national [Belorussian] literature."[74] Furthermore, the value of their work is praised in terms that are surprisingly nationalistic:

> Every people has poets who . . . so profoundly and strikingly, so frankly express their secret thoughts and dreams, that it appears as if they themselves are the soul of the people. For us Belorussians . . . [these poets

are] Ya. Kupala and Ya. Kolas. The lasting value of their
work is that they filled our hearts with ardent love for our
native land and its people [emphasis added].75

Enhancing the significance of these assertions is the fact that the
"heroes," literary or otherwise, presented to the public in any newspaper in the Soviet have undoubtedly received Party approval before-
hand. For two such examples of Belorussian nationality consciousness to have made it past this screening process would seem to indicate a recognition of their importance to the Belorussian nationality,
an importance that evidently cannot be safely ignored.

A few of the many observations made in the press of the BSSR
on the anniversaries of the births of Kupala and Kolas will serve to
suggest their influence and outlook. Among the more salient points
made concerning Yanka Kupala were that "nationality" (narodnost)
formed the foundation for his work and that he was responsible for
bringing Belorussian literature to the attention of Maxim Gorky, the
guiding force of Soviet literature in the immediate post-1917 period.76
As for Yakub Kolas, it was stated that the history of the Belorussian
nationality was reflected in his poetry "through the prism of his private perceptions" and that he was a "consistent defender of the social
and national interest of the Belorussian people."77 Though efforts
were made to establish their involvement in the "mutual enrichment"
process of Soviet culture by citing, for example, Kupala's debt to
Russian literature78 and the influence upon Kolas of Russian, Ukrainian,
and Uzbek culture,79 the thrust of the coverage concerning Kupala
and Kolas established both their own nationality consciousness and
the vitality of the Belorussian nationality that they represented.

This affirmation of Belorussian nationality consciousness in
the face of the restrictions cited earlier confirms the validity of an
observation that the self-identification of the Belorussians is the key
to group cohesiveness. As long as they continue to consider themselves different from Russians, Ukrainians, and others, this distinctiveness will continue to be reflected, however sparingly, in the
local press with indications that the essence of the Belorussian nationality, its ethnic self-identity, is very much alive and quite possibly growing stronger with every passing year.

THE IMPACT OF SOVIET FEDERALISM

In summary, therefore, the choice of a federal political structure
for the Soviet Union appears to have guaranteed a prolonged existence
for the Belorussian nationality. This concretization of the idea of
"socialist in content, national in form" has allowed the Belorussian

nationality to "flourish" with each of its tangible characteristics (language, territory, and economy) drawing strength from the other two. When language was assailed by assimilationist pressure, it found reinforcement in the territorial principle that guaranteed its continued use for governmental and instruction purposes, and in an economy that made the unwritten slogan "made in the BSSR" a source of nationality pride. When the territorial structure was threatened, it was bolstered by the reaffirmation of the principle that those whose common origin is symbolized by a common language have the right— the right of self-determination proclaimed by Lenin—to a nationality territory of their own. Finally, the sense of nationality identity fostered by a common language and distinct territory made centralists reluctant to ignore the needs of the Belorussian economy. But underlying all of these factors is the stubborn self-awareness of being Belorussian, which was reinforced by the interaction of the main attributes. Even if a competing sense of being Soviet were to gain ground, it is our belief that no more than an accommodation would take place. Belorussians would acculturate, adopting the Soviet culture without giving up their own culture, but not assimilate. So far this accommodation extends only to a sense of Soviet citizenship, as exemplified by the following: "I am a Belorussian and I take pride in this. I have an everlasting love for my maternal land. Therefore with great pride I call myself a citizen of a great state—the Union of Soviet Socialist Republics [emphasis added].[80]

In attempting to weigh the significance of each factor in the struggle between integrative pressures and nationality consciousness, it is clear that the key to this interaction is the essence, the ethnic self-awareness, of the Belorussian nationality because:

[i]n the final analysis, the coincidence of the customary tangible attributes of nationality, such as common language . . . is not determinative. The prime requisite is subjective and consists of the self-identification of people with a group—its past, its present, and, most important, its destiny. [emphasis added].[81]

However, it still remains for us to offer some ranking of the importance of the various influences playing upon that essence: the attributes— language, economy, and national territory—of the Belorussian nationality, the actors—the Party and Komsomol—in the struggle between integrative pressures and nationality consciousness, and the context— federalism and the Soviet West—of the aforementioned struggle.

If this task of ranking were approached by working back from direct influences to more indirect influences and, finally, to some "prime mover," the attributes of the Belorussian nationality, though

127

clearly the most immediate influences upon its essence, would be
found, in turn, to be shaped by the context in which they operate,
especially by the system of Soviet federalism. However, Soviet
federalism itself is the creation of the Party,[82] which must therefore
be classified as the long-sought "prime mover." Attributing such a
role to the Party would not be unusual since it is the self-proclaimed
"leading element" of Soviet society. This, however, may overem-
phasize the significance of the Party.

A more useful method for determining the relative importance
of each of the above-mentioned influences is to consider them as parts
of an interlocking system and then evaluate what the effect would be
of replacing or altering any one of them, attaching the greatest significance to those elements that affect the essence in a positive fashion.
By pursuing this line of investigation, the Party can be shown to rate
as probably the least important positive influence upon the essence
of the Belorussian nationality, since the Party's efforts are directed
toward the "merger of nationalities" and it therefore seeks to monitor
and/or restrain that essence rather than promote it. The next rung
up the ladder is the economy of the BSSR because, despite its contribution to the sense of relative deprivation that reinforces the essence
of the Belorussian nationality, it could just as easily be a capitalist
rather than a socialist economy, or perhaps one run directly by Moscow
without the Belorussian Gosplan (State Planning Committee) as intermediary; this would not significantly affect Belorussian self-identity.
Even the language attribute, most visible symbol of the Belorussian
nationality, could be altered without seriously undercutting Belorussian
self-awareness. This leaves federalism and the territorial attribute
inextricably linked, because the Belorussian nationality territory is
the concrete representation of the Soviet federal system. They will
therefore be treated as one influence and accorded the status of primary influence upon the essence of the Belorussian nationality. To
objections that Soviet federalism is a sham and that the Soviet Union
is in reality a unitary state, rendering the existence of nationality
territories irrelevant, the following observation may provide an answer:

> national governments, even when impotent, are known
> from historical experience to arouse strong feelings of
> loyalty among both their officials and subjects. . . . The
> fact that the [Belorussian] Republic is a Soviet creation,
> and that its government enjoys no meaningful authority,
> probably does not make it any less real for the [Belo-
> russians], and especially for the [Belorussian] intelli-
> gentsia.[83]

Soviet federalism and its creature, the Belorussian nationality territory, provide the proper atmosphere to nurture the Belorussian sense of nationality self-identity.

Looking back at the Belorussian nationality that entered the Union of Soviet Socialist Republics in December 1922, and comparing it with the one that exists today, it is apparent that the net effect of 50 years of Soviet federalism with the Party as taskmaster has been the formation of an initially splintered, economically weak, and illiterate nationality into an economically advanced, and advancing, nationality, with its own intelligentsia, cultural centers, literary language, and sense of common historical fate. To paraphrase one Western historian, one might say that Soviet federalism, though designed to mollify ethnonationalism, has, in effect, intensified it and provided it with institutional outlets.[84]

What do these observations about the Belorussian nationality augur for the Soviet nationality question in general and for its outcome in the Soviet West in particular? As long as the prevalent tendency is to emphasize the traits that divide rather than those that unite, the Soviet Union will continue to be made up of separate nationalities each of which possesses the necessary common psychological bond to hold itself together and exhibit vitality in spite of and perhaps because of integrative pressure, while, at the same time, the Party will persevere in its efforts to foster the concept of a supraethnic Soviet nation. As for the Soviet West, if the Belorussian press is any indication, it will remain a collection of jealously guarded ethnic fiefdoms, for there is no sign of even a nascent Soviet Western common identity.[85]

NOTES

1. Merle Fainsod, How Russia is Ruled, (Cambridge, Mass.: Harvard University Press, 1967), p. 363.

2. See for example, Leonid Brezhnev, "O piatidesiatiletii soiuza sovetskikh sotsialisticheskikh respublik," Sovetskaia Belorussiia [hereafter abbreviated as Sov. Bel.], December 22, 1972, p. 2.

3. Theodore Shabad, "Soviet is Pressing the Blending of Its 100 Nationalities," New York Times, July 31, 1972, p. 2.

4. Itogi vsesoiuznoi perepisi naseleniia 1970 goda. Tom. IV. Natsional'nyi sostav naseleniia SSSR (Moscow: Statistika, 1973); and Itogi vsesoiuznoi perepisi naseleniia 1959 goda: Belorusskaia SSR (Moscow: Gosstatizdat, 1963) [hereafter abbreviated as Itogi 1970 or Itogi 1959]. Narodnoe khoziastvo SSSR, various years (Moscow: Statistika, various years) [hereafter abbreviated as Nar. khoz. SSSR]. Also Narodnoe khoziastvo BSSR, 1971 (Minsk: Belarus, 1972) [hereafter abbreviated as Nar. khoz. BSSR].

5. See, for example, Walker Connor, "Nation-Building or Nation-Destroying?," World Politics, 24, No. 3 (April 1972), pp. 319-55; Vernon Van Dyke, "Self-Determination and Minority Rights," International Studies Quarterly, 13, No. 3 (September 1969), pp. 223-53; Joseph Nye, "Comparative Regional Integration: Concept and Measurement," International Organization, 22, No. 4 (Autumn 1968), pp. 855-80; and Claude Ake, A Theory of Political Integration (Homewood, Ill.: Dorsey Press, 1967).

6. Derived from definitions of "nation" and "state" in Jack C. Plano and Roy Olton, The International Relations Dictionary (New York: Holt, Rinehart & Winston, 1969).

7. Joseph Stalin, Marxism and the National Question (Moscow: Foreign Language Publishing House, 1950), p. 16.

8. M. A. Sverdlin and P. M. Rogachev, "O poniatii 'natsiia'" Voprosy istorii, No. 1 (January 1966).

9. Walker Connor, "Nationalism Reconsidered" (Paper presented at the 1971 Annual Meeting of the Northeast Political Science Association), p. 31.

10. Connor, "Nation-Building," p. 338.

11. Connor, "Nationalism Reconsidered," p. 32.

12. Ibid. p. 7.

13. Zvi Gitelman, "The Jews," Problems of Communism, 16, No. 5 (September-October 1967), p. 100.

14. Van Dyke, "Self-Determination," p. 226.

15. John N. Hazard, "Fifty Years of the Soviet Federation," Canadian Slavonic Papers, 14, No. 4 (Winter 1972), p. 587, and M. Shkliar, "Splochenie," Sov. Bel., 10 October 1972, p. 2.

16. V. Borushko and A. Kukevich, "Vsemirno-istoricheskoe znachenie obrazovaniia SSSR," Sov. Bel., 21 December 1972, p. 3; Brezhnev, "O piatidesiatiletii," p. 2; Shkliar, "Splochenie," p. 2.

17. This capsule description of the history of Belorussia is drawn from Ivan S. Lubachko, Belorussia Under Soviet Rule, 1917-1957 (Lexington: University Press of Kentucky, 1972), and Nicholas P. Vakar, Belorussia: The Making of a Nation (Cambridge, Mass.: Harvard University Press, 1956).

18. Lubachko, Belorussia, p. 4.

19. Rein Taagepera, "Dissimilarities Among the Northwestern Soviet Republics," in Problems of Mininations: Baltic Perspectives, ed. Arvids Ziedonis, et al. (San Jose, Ca.: Association for Advancement of Baltic Studies, 1973), p. 77.

20. "Narod i partiia ediny," Sov. Bel., 19 July 1972, p. 2.

21. "Vystuplenie tovarishcha P.M. Masherova," Sov. Bel., 22 December 1972, p. 6.

22. "Kompartiia Belorussii v tsifrakh," Kommunist Belorussii, No. 8, (August 1968), p. 36.

23. Itogi . . . 1970, Table 2, p. 13.

24. Ibid., Table 9, p. 193.

25. Ethnic composition of BCP's Party Bureau calculated from B.S.E.: Ezhegodnik, 1971 (Moscow, 1972), p. 124 and Deputaty verkhovnogo soveta SSSR: sedmoi soyuz (Moscow, 1966), pp. 530 and 537-8.

26. S. Pochanin and V. Bobkov, "Pod znamenem proletarskogo internatsionalizma," Znamia iunosti, 21 November 1972, p. 2.

27. Charlotte Saikowski and Leo Gruliow, eds., Current Soviet Policies, IV (New York: Columbia University Press, 1962), p. 103.

28. Brezhnev, "O piatidesiatiletii," p. 3.

29. As quoted in Vladimir Podrez, "Vospitanie kadrov—boevaia zadacha komsomola," Znamia iunosti, November 23, 1972, p. 2.

30. J. V. Stalin, Works (Moscow: Foreign Languages Publishing House, 1952), V, p. 49.

31. Nicholas P. Vakar, "The Belorussian People Between Nationhood and Extinction," in Ethnic Minorities in the Soviet Union, ed. Erich Goldhagen (N.Y.: Praeger, 1968) p. 218.

32. "O vozrastnoi, strukture, urovne obrazovaniia, national'-nom sostave, iazykh: sredstv sushchestvovaniia naseleniia SSSR po dannym vsesoiuznoi perepisi naseleniia na 15 ianvaria 1970 goda," Sov. Bel., April 17, 1971, p. 3.

33. Calculated from the 1970 census. See Itogi 1970, p. 9 (Table 1) and p. 192 (Table 9).

34. A. A. Rakov, Naselenie BSSR (Minsk: Nauka i Tekhnika, 1969), p. 123.

35. "Events in Byelorussia," Journal of Byelorussian Studies (London) 2, No. 4 (1972), p. 419.

36. Roman Szporluk, "The Press in Belorussia, 1955-1965," Soviet Studies 18, No. 4 (April 1967), p. 488.

37. For example, Article 25 of the Belorussian constitution stipulates that all laws will be published in Belorussian, while Article 96 guarantees education in Belorussian. See Constitution of the Belorussian Soviet Socialist Republic (New York: American Russian Institute, 1950), pp. 4, 13.

38. Connor, "Nationalism Reconsidered," p. 6.

39. Concerning the early cession of territory, see E. H. Carr, Socialism in One Country, II (London: Penguin Books, 1970), p. 281; on the territory acquired from Poland, see Vakar, Belorussia, p. 207.

40. Hazard, "Soviet Federation," p. 589.

41. "Belorussiia: 50 let v bratskoi sem'e narodov SSSR," Sov. Bel., 26 Nov. 1972, pp. 2-3.

42. Borushko and Kukevich, "Vsemirno-istoricheskoe znachenie," p. 3.

43. P. Dodin, "V sem'e edinoi," Sov. Bel., January 21, 1972, p. 1.

44. V. Borushko, "Sila slivaiushchaia natsii," Sov. Bel., October 20, 1972, p. 2.

45. For a more detailed discussion of the concept of "relative deprivation" and its consequences, see Ted Robert Gurr, Why Men Rebel (Princeton, N.J.: Princeton University Press, 1970), pp. 24, 105.

46. Masherov, "Sozidaiushchaia," p. 2.

47. See: V. N. Bandera ano Z. L. Melnyk, eds. The Soviet Economy in Regional Perspective (New York: Praeger, 1973).

48. Brezhnev, "O piatidesiatiletii," p. 5.

49. Brian Silver, "Levels of Sociocultural Development Among Soviet Nationalities: A Partial Test of the Equalization Hypothesis" (Paper presented at the 69th Annual Meeting of the American Political Science Association, New Orleans, September 4-8, 1973), Table 11.

50. "Narod i partiia," p. 2.

51. Connor, "Nation-Building," p. 353.

52. S. Azduni, "Sovetskii narod—novaia istoricheskaia obshchnost' liudei," Sov. Bel., November 15, 1972, p. 2.

53. Azduni, "Sovetskii narod," p. 3.

54. S. I. Ozhegov, Slovar' russkogo iazyka (Moscow: Sovetskaia entsiklopedia, 1968), p. 370.

55. Ibid., pp. 386, 378.

56. John A. Armstrong, "The Ethnic Scene in the Soviet Union: The View of the Dictatorship," in Ethnic Minorities in the Soviet Union, ed. Erich Goldhagen (N.Y.: Praeger, 1968), p. 6; Silver, "Sociocultural Development," p. 10.

57. Nar. khoz. BSSR, p. 6.

58. Calculated from the 1970 census, Itogi 1970, p. 9 (Table 1) and p. 192 (Table 9).

59. Taagepera, "Dissimilarities," p. 10.

60. "Belorussiia: 50 let," p. 2.

61. Calculated from the 1970 census, Itogi 1970, p. 480, (Table 41).

62. Ibid.

63. Connor, "Nation-Building," p. 349.

64. Connor, "Nationalism Reconsidered," p. 27.

65. Iu V. Bromlei, "Leninizm i osnovnye tendentsii etnicheskikh protsessov v SSSR," Sovetskaia etnografiia, No. 1 (1970), p. 13.

66. Masherov, "Sozidaiushchaia," p. 2.

67. "Belorussiia: 50 let," p. 2.

68. Ibid., p. 3.

69. Ibid.

70. "Belorussiia vstrechaet svoikh olimpiitsev," Sov. Bel., September 15, 1972, p. 3.

71. "Olimpiiskii vzlet," Sov. Bel., September 15, 1972, p. 3.

72. "Istoriia glazami khudozhnika," Sov. Bel., November 1, 1972, p. 2.

73. See, for example, Anthony Adamovich, Opposition to Sovietization in Belorussian Literature, 1917-1957 (New York: Scarecrow Press for the Institute for the Study of the USSR, 1958).

74. Iu. Pshirkov, "Uchit'sia u zhizni . . . ne pokladaia ruk," Sov. Bel., November 3, 1972, p. 1.

75. M. Mikheichik, "S liubov'iu k cheloveku," Sov. Bel., November 3, 1972, p. 1.

76. Vladimir Iurevich, "Pervaia iz vershin," Sov. Bel., July 7, 1972, p. 1.

77. Pshirkov, "Uchit'sia u zhizni," pp. 1-2.

78. Iurevich, "Pervaia iz vershin," p. 1.

79. A. Kapustin, I. Podorozhanskii, and A. Butevich, "Pesni bratstva nad Nemanom," Sov. Bel., September 19, 1972, p. 1.

80. M. Sokolov, "Gordost' nasha-strana sovetov," Sov. Bel., July 30, 1972, p. 2.

81. Walker Connor, "Self-Determination: The New Phase," World Politics, 20, No. 1 (October 1967), p. 30.

82. See Robert Conquest, Soviet Nationalities Policy in Practice (London: Bodley Head, 1967), p. 27.

83. Richard Pipes, "'Solving' the Nationality Problem," Problems of Communism, 16, No. 5 (September-October 1967), p. 128. Though Professor Pipes used the Uzbeks as his example, we have substituted the Belorussians to make our point.

84. Ibid.

85. During 1972, each of the 14 other union republics was featured in one issue of Sovetskaia Belorussiia (the issues for each of the republics of the Soviet West were as follows: May 21, 1972—the Ukraine; September 10, 1972—Lithuania; September 24, 1972—Moldavia; October 8, 1972—Latvia; and we were unable to locate the issue covering Estonia). The format for these special treatments was usually the same. On the front page there was a combination travelogue and capsule history of the subject republic since it became part of the USSR prepared by BELTA (The Belorussian Telegraphic Agency). Inside there were usually two articles, one written by a Belorussian and one by someone from the subject republic describing examples of cooperation between the BSSR and the subject republic. This cooperation was always couched in terms of the "family of fraternal republics" and never gave any evidence of any special Soviet Western common identity.

9

**YOUTH OF THE
LITHUANIAN SSR AND
THE QUESTION OF
NATIONALITY
DIVISIVENESS**
Norman Kass

The assertion of a vital sense of nationality by young people within the Lithuanian SSR constitutes a major force in the expression of the cultural situation prevailing within Lithuania. This assertion is discernible on two distinct levels of interaction. The first involves such officially sanctioned groups as the Communist Youth League (Komsomol) and individual theatrical, artistic, and cultural entourages, and their attempts to counteract regional integrative pressures exerted by the leadership of the Komsomol, the Communist Party, and the Ministry of Culture of the Lithuanian SSR. The second level of interaction, largely lacking the organizational structure of the first, is characterized by a rejection of established means of expressing the vitality of the nationality and by a subsequent quest for alternative ways through which such vitality can be expressed. The purpose of this inquiry will be to locate and determine the manifestations of integrative pressures and nationality divisiveness within the Komsomol and the various cultural and artistic groups within the Lithuanian SSR. By integrative pressures we mean a systematic and sustained effort, on the part of the Komsomol, the Communist Party, and governmental authorities, to incorporate the Lithuanian SSR into a single, harmonious Soviet cultural and national entity. Divisiveness here refers to the centrifugal tendencies, both deliberate and unintended, on the part of Lithuanian youth, the thrust of which aims at the assertion and perpetuation of nationality self-awareness.

As a means of examining the interaction within the two levels noted above, evidence from the Komsomol newspaper of the Lithuanian SSR, Komsomol'skaia pravda (from the period November 1972 through February 1973), and from the Republic newspaper, Sovetskaia Litva (covering the months of August through November 1972), is evaluated in terms of the following criteria: (1) space/coverage devoted to the Lithuanian SSR as a distinct cultural entity; (2) the source of the item, that is, located within the Lithuanian SSR (ELTA) or transmitted from outside (TASS); (3) the position and nationality of the writer as well as the agency which he represents; and (4) the tone and style in which a particular item has been written. Additional research materials include issues of the Chronicle of the Catholic Church of Lithuania (samizdat) and a variety of publications from Lithuanian emigre sources in the United States.

With specific regard to the second level of interaction noted earlier (rejection of established means of expressing nationality consciousness and the subsequent quest for alternative ways through which such vitality can be exhibited), assessments of the degree of nationality divisiveness reflected in particular items are based on the following considerations: (1) the pervasiveness, repetitiveness, and significance of the event; (2) the extent to which an event falls within an organizational framework, such as that of the Roman Catholic Church; (3) whether a particular phenomenon is depicted as a direct challenge or threat to integrative pressures; and (4) the extent and type of response which the description of a particular event elicits from the readership. Finally, an effort will be made to establish the extent to which the youth of the Lithuanian SSR join with other societal sectors in the expression of nationality identity. Conversely, the degree to which Lithuanian youth behave independently of and in conflict with other social units will be pursued.

At the outset it is useful to note the sizable increase in the number of Lithuanians in their titular republic during the period 1959-1970. According to Soviet census data, the number of Lithuanians in the Lithuanian SSR increased some 16 percent in the 11-year intercensal period. The corresponding figures for increases during this same period in the number of the titular nationality within two other republics of the Soviet West—Estonia and Latvia—are 3.6 percent and 3.4 percent, respectively.[1] The census data also disclose that the Lithuanian SSR is approximately 80 percent Lithuanian, while the percentages of the titular nationality of the Estonian SSR and Latvian SSR are 68 and 57 percent, respectively.[2] Clearly, compared to the other Baltic republics, Lithuania has maintained a high degree of ethnic homogeneity. The sharp increase in the number of Lithuanians in the Lithuanian SSR attests to the significance of Lithuanian youth as a social group instrumental in expressing nationality stamina both now and in the years ahead since even a moderately high rate of growth results in a large percentage of younger age groups in the population.

A concern with the important role played by youth in the assertion of Lithuanian nationality consciousness suggests inquiry into the activities of the Komsomol within the Lithuanian SSR. As a major force in the direction of cultural and national integration, the Komsomol is closely patterned after the Communist party. Through a network of primary organizations, regional and city committees, and a Central Committee, the Komsomol serves as a structure for the preservation and reinforcement of ideological conformity. Membership is considered essential for acceptance into the ranks of the Communist party and, consequently, becomes a prerequisite for a successful career. With its wide variety of social and cultural programs and endless campaigns to fit the young into the mold of the exemplary Soviet citizen, the Komsomol faces no rivalry from any other officially recognized organization. Yet, acknowledging the strong pressure toward homogenization that the Komsomol can and does exert upon the youth, the emphasis that it places upon the thorough ideological training of its members, and the function that it has as a proving ground for acceptance into the Communist party, one could ask if the Komsomol does not also serve as a forum for the expression of nationality identity. In other words, do the lofty goals espoused in official Komsomol proclamations undergo mutation when confronted by the social and political conditions within the Lithuanian SSR?

Perhaps the most striking manifestation of this cleavage between the realms of ideals and reality is the pervasive, persistent, and sustained unresponsiveness on the part of Lithuanian youth to the vast array of programs initiated by the Komsomol leadership. Moreover, this apathy toward Komsomol programs, readily apparent from even a cursory survey of official Komsomol publications, has manifested itself on all levels of the organization and in a multitude of ways, including a decline in readership of the Komsomol press, poor attendance at meetings, and a disregard for Komsomol-sponsored programs. Thus, readers learn of concern caused by a decrease in the number of subscriptions to the Komsomol press. An editorial comment appearing in Komsomol'skaia pravda in November 1972, bemoans the fact that the readership which the newspaper has is less than it was a year ago in certain areas of the Republic.[3] Further evidence of the declining interest in the Komsomol press comes from an instructor at Vilnius State University. Describing the rigors of the final-examination period in the early part of January 1973, the instructor regrets that his students do not read the local press and are therefore unable to answer the current-events questions which he presents to them.[4] Probably the most telling sign of the Lithuanian youth's indifference toward the local Komsomol press appears in the lack of response to the controversial news stories expressly soliciting the reactions of the readership. One particular feature, regularly commented upon in Komsomol'skaia pravda, appearing under the heading "Priglashenie k tantsu" ("Invitation to Dance"), is quite critical of the modern styles of dance which many young Lithuanians seem to have acquired from the West. The strong criticism of "decadent" Western musical trends seizing Lithuania's youth has been answered in the press with silence. Not a single attempt by Lithuania's youth to justify its subculture surfaces in the Komsomol press in the four-month period surveyed. An undoubtedly unintended stimulus to youth's continued apathy toward the Komsomol press was contained in a letter to the editor of Komsomol'skaia pravda appearing on January 14, 1973. The author of the letter, a state farm worker named A. Simonavichius, remarked that subscribers to Komsomol'skaia pravda are not receiving their copies at all, or only after long delays. In response to the letter, the editor ruefully remarks that while postal authorities are aware of the problems encountered in the delivery of the paper, they have yet to undertake any concrete measures to improve existing distribution procedures.[5] Apparently the unappealing quality of the paper's contents, as evidenced by the decline in readership in various parts of the Lithuanian SSR, together with the unpredictability of its arrival, reinforce the indifference of Lithuania's youth towards the Komsomol press.

Attendance at Komsomol functions also serves as a measure of youth's enthusiasm for officially sponsored activities. There is recurrent evidence that participation among Lithuania's young people at Komsomol meetings falls below the expectations of the leadership.[6] Meetings are said to be boring and to belabor ideas which have grown monotonous over time.[7]

Countless examples of youth's lack of involvement in the programs of Lithuanian Komsomol may be ascertained from the press. A recently instituted program encouraging regional integration and subordination to a central authority further illustrates the over-all process of disengagement on the part of Lithuanian youth. The new program, established in early 1972, is known by the initials GTO, an acronym for Gotov k trudu i oborone SSSR ("Ready for the Labor and Defense of the USSR"). Designed to raise the level of military preparedness and athletic prowess among the young, GTO, a Union-wide program, relies for its success upon the support which it receives from the Komsomol. However, the success of GTO's sports program is impeded to a significant extent by the lack of enthusiasm for it on the part of Lithuanian Komsomol members. As a result of such unresponsiveness, many of the high standards of success established at the republic and Union-wide levels have been eroded on the local level. Describing the relaxation of GTO requirements in the Lithuanian SSR, one writer expresses concern that the entire program will become nothing more than the formality of issuing badges (znachki), and certificates of completion of the GTO program to those who do not deserve to have them. The title of the author's article, "Will Paper-Badge Recipients Appear?" accentuates the process by which an ambitious scheme promoted from above turns into a frail entity whose chances for growth are impaired by the indifference with which youth greets it.[8]

While the Komsomol press tends to dwell mainly upon individual primary organizations associated with schools, factories, and collective farms throughout the Lithuanian SSR as the units where unresponsiveness to Komsomol programs is likely to emerge, there are indications of indifference in Komsomol echelons above the primary level. These indications are generally referred to as manifestations of "formalism," which, in Soviet parlance, connotes an inflexibility stemming from unwillingness to discard established policies for the sake of experimenting with new and uncertain ones. Formalism is often cited as a reason for the poor performance of Komsomol members and the stagnation of Komsomol activities. For example, a very recent article in the Lithuanian press explicitly criticizes the Vilnius Regional Committee of the Komsomol for its mechanical treatment of programs that were submitted to it by the Komsomol Central Committee. It was alleged that the Vilnius Regional Committee, instead of dispensing instructions and guidance for the implementation of the programs received from the Central Committee (no specific programs cited), simply made copies of them and summarily transmitted them to subordinate echelons.[9] Such activity on the part of the Regional Committee was viewed with disfavor largely because of the example of apathy that it provided the primary Komsomol committees under its jurisdiction. "How," asks the critic of the Vilnius Regional Committee, "can one demand very much of the lower echelon Komsomol organizations and individual members if this is how a regional committee behaves."[10] The "formalism" of the Komsomol leadership may well lead to further unresponsiveness to, and disengagement from, the programs that the leadership attempts to conduct in a sterile and stereotyped fashion.

To what extent does the display of apathy represent a rebellion against an established order and to what extent does it comprise a conscious and deliberate attempt at asserting nationality consciousness? Apathy toward a pressure for integration and homogenization, whether or not deriving from a conscious effort to seek nationality identity, is, in and of itself, a retarding force in integration and, therefore, a positive element in the reinforcement of nationality consciousness. Moreover, having developed from a desire to rebel against the integrative pressure of the Komsomol, apathy perhaps evolved into a conscious and deliberate attempt by youth within the Lithuanian SSR to find, within the framework of an integrative structure, the means for expressing nationality identity. Thus, the Komsomol of the Lithuanian SSR emerges as an arena for the interaction of centrifugal and centripetal forces, with nationality consciousness surfacing as a prominent outcome of this interplay.

In addition to the Komsomol, a multitude of cultural, theatrical, and artistic groups functioning within the Republic provide valuable channels through which Lithuanian youth is able to assert itself. The Lithuanian Komsomol press does not portray cultural activities undertaken by young people exclusively in terms of the nationality distinctiveness that such activities encourage and sustain. Rather, cultural events appear to be of three basic sorts. First, a variety of cultural events are clearly integrative in nature, designed to emphasize the unity and brotherhood of the diverse, ethnically distinctive groups making up a single Soviet culture, and stressing its integrative impact on Lithuanian life. Thus, in an article discussing the performances of the National Ensemble of Song and Dance at Vilnius State University, the concept of unity is evoked by noting that the theme of the Ensemble's performances is "the indestructible friendship of the peoples of our country."[11] In a similar way, the cultural program of the Vilnius Pedagogical Institute, which has established a series of "international weeks" for each of the Soviet republics, was undertaken in commemoration of the fiftieth anniversary of the formation of the Soviet Union.[12] At an evening get-together held in the Prenai region for young teachers and Komsomol representatives, among the events in the program was a quiz game called "Do you know the USSR?"[13] At times the integrative theme reflects a bilateral basis, involving an exchange of cultural activity between two republics, such as the ties between Lithuanian and Moldavian literature and the efforts to translate the literature of one republic into the language of the other.[14] The cultural ties between Lithuania and Moldavia as depicted in that article are subsumed under an integrative theme of showing the growth and cultural "blossoming" of both republics following their entry into the Soviet Union.

A second category of cultural activities places great importance upon the uniqueness of the Lithuanian SSR and, in certain instances, makes no reference to Lithuania's position either as one of 15 Union republics comprising the USSR or as one of the six republics within the Soviet West. Within this category two different attitudes toward culture as manifestation of Lithuanian vitality and individuality seem to be evident. Some of these depict cultural interaction between the Lithuanian SSR and other regions of the Soviet West and Eastern Europe. Illustrative of such cultural ties are the efforts that have recently been made to expand the current series of theatrical performances between the Lithuanian Academy of Drama and the Weimar National Theatre of the German Democratic Republic.[15] A concert given in Czechoslovakia by the members of the Vilnius Youth Choir "Azhyoliukas," performing Lithuanian national songs, is a further example of cultural activity undertaken by young Lithuanian artists to express and assert nationality distinctiveness.[16] Occasionally,

the singularity of Lithuanian culture emerges as a result of international competition at which Lithuanian performers excel. Reports of
such competition, manifestly proud in their tone, emphasize the Lithuanian performers and their works and accomplishments.[17]

Other cultural events accentuating Lithuanian nationality uniqueness deal with artistic, theatrical, and musical programs taking place
within the Lithuanian SSR which do not involve interaction with areas
outside the Republic. Theatrical competition occurs among young
Lithuanian actors, and at subsequent conferences the results are
discussed. This allows young performers to exchange views with
more experienced artists and stage directors of the Lithuanian SSR,
and, apparently, fosters the strengthening of cultural identity through
an interaction of different social groups within the Republic.[18] An
additional and rather revealing event concerning culture as a vehicle
for the furthering of nationality consciousness in the Lithuanian SSR
is an article discussing a young Lithuanian actor, Pranas Piauokas,
who is reported to have been accepted as a performer at the Shiauliai
Drama Theatre as a step toward bringing about a rejuvenation
(omolozhenie) of the theatre and its repertoire.[19] Here again the
interaction between Lithuanian youth and an older group of cultural
leaders with whom they deal emerges as a vibrant means for the
expression of cultural distinctiveness. Similarly, on an intrarepublic
basis, the Komsomol press, reporting the opening of an art exhibit
displaying works of students at the Art Institute of the Lithuanian
SSR, specifically mentions the theme of Lithuanian rural life.[20] This
theme provides the residents of Vilnius with the opportunity to enjoy
an important aspect of their cultural tradition. Failure to mention
any indebtedness to Russian literature in a critique of the works of
four young Lithuanian poets may serve as the final and most striking
illustration of cultural events providing a means of asserting nationality
consciousness.[21]

The third category of cultural pursuits, and by far the most
frequently encountered, combines elements of nationality assertiveness and divisiveness, on the one hand, and pressures for integration,
on the other. While the overall impression of such items varies
with the amount of space and detail devoted to each of these two elements, a precise evaluation of the significance ascribed to integration
and divisiveness is often virtually impossible to establish.

The merger or juxtaposition of integrative and divisive themes
within a single cultural phenomenon seems at times to arise from
one theme being the unintended and unforeseen consequence or rever-
beration of the other. A close contact has developed, for example,
between young Lithuanian and Latvian poets as a result of the integrative pressures exerted by the fiftieth anniversary celebration of the
formation of the Soviet Union.[22] Stretching beyond the campaign to

show Lithuanian and Latvian cultures as closely interwoven into a single Soviet cultural fabric, the close ties between the young poets of the two Baltic republics have apparently provided Lithuanian poetry with a major means of expression. Thus, what began as an integrative pursuit promoted by the Ministry of Culture was, perhaps through over-zealousness, converted into a channel for expressing Lithuanian vitality and distinctiveness. Conversely, certain cultural events in the Lithuanian SSR, clearly divisive in nature, pale as an expression of nationality consciousness and acquire the characteristic of an attempt at cultural integration. Thus, an exhibition of Lithuanian artistic traditions at the Kaunas Sculpture Gallery attracted visitors from all parts of the Lithuanian SSR, as well as from neighboring republics and other socialist countries.[23] Clearly, the event as depicted up to this point would be interpreted as showing Lithuanian nationality divisiveness. There was, however, a noticeable lack of attendance on the part of Kaunas residents and particularly of school children. The absence of Kaunas residents from a display of national art works might be explained by their perception of such an event as pressure for integration rather than as an outlet for nationality consciousness. What began as a cultural event clearly showing cultural distinctiveness became one of blurred dimensions, where the assertion of nationality identity and pressures for cultural integration exist and interact side by side.

The three categories of cultural events presented above—those distinctively integrative in character, those emphasizing nationality divisiveness, and those embracing both integrative and divisive tendencies—differ in terms of the extent to which they provide an understanding of the interaction among different social strata within the Lithuanian SSR and between Lithuanian cultural groups and those elsewhere in the Soviet West and Eastern Europe. Reports stressing the integrative pressure of cultural activity in which Lithuanian youth is involved are the same ones in which the concept of group interaction is almost entirely absent. For example, proclamations of "the indestructible friendship of the people of our country" rarely mention the kinds of people with whom Lithuanian cultural groups come in contact during their tours as representatives of the Soviet culture.[24] This striking absence of any reference to group interaction may well be attributed to a preoccupation with the utopian idea of a single Soviet entity and the concomitant denial of any cultural heterogeneity.

In contrast to the negligible group interaction discernible in cultural events of a purely integrative function, those cultural events reflecting divisiveness or a combination of divisiveness and integrative pressure, often reveal clear indications of interaction among various social groups. Interactions among the nationalities residing within the Lithuanian SSR—Lithuanians, Poles, Belorussians, Ukrainians,

Jews, and Latvians, to cite the major groups in order of numerical size—do not surface in the portrayal of cultural activity in which Lithuanian youth is engaged. One does not find reference to concerts, art exhibits, or poetry recitals, for instance, which, by their content, are clearly designed for a particular nationality within the Lithuanian SSR. Cultural activity involving Lithuanian youth with other areas of the Soviet West and Eastern Europe, contains no evidence that a particular performance or exhibit is intended for any nationality or nationalities in the area in which it is held. Rather, interaction between youth groups of the Lithuanian SSR engaged in cultural activity and other social groups, whether within the Republic or in other areas of the Soviet West and Eastern Europe, crystallizes in one or both of the following ways: first, on the basis of specific cultural groups sharing a common medium of expression, whether art, drama, music, or literature; and second, on the basis of age groups, involving youth and those imprecisely defined as "representatives of the older age group."[25] Both types of interaction emerge either as an expression of nationality uniqueness or as a source of centrifugal force confronted by an intense centripetal counterpressure.

In addition to the Komsomol and cultural programs that are officially recognized and encouraged by the Party and government authorities of the Lithuanian SSR, another category of youth activity exists in the form of an independent quest for nationality and cultural identity. This can be examined under three topical headings:
(1) The Roman Catholic Church and its role as a cultural entity;
(2) the adoption of Western culture;
(3) the tendency toward antisocial behavior.

Historically, the Catholic Church in Lithuania has served as a center for religious worship and is a basic element in Lithuanian cultural life. The prominent role of the Church in art, music, and literature has created a situation in which the themes of religion and culture have been intertwined over time. The following of the Church in Lithuania on the eve of the country's annexation into the Soviet Union was very large: "In 1940, when the Soviet Russians occupied Lithuania, of the more than 3,000,000 inhabitants 85.5 percent were Catholic. . . . Lithuanians comprised 80.6 percent of the population; 94.4 percent of them were Catholic."[26] While no precise figures indicating the present number of Catholics within the Lithuanian SSR are available, evidence suggests that over the past three decades the emphasis on atheistic indoctrination has forced a decline in the organizational structure of the Catholic Church in Lithuania. There has been a sharp decline in the number of bishops, priests, and seminarians, with the strength of the Church in these categories in 1971 equalling about one-half the number of clerics in 1940. Likewise, the number of churches and seminaries has decreased by approximately one-half over the same period.[27]

Despite the numerical decrease in the institutions promoting Church activities and in the leadership of the Catholic Church within the Lithuanian SSR, the Church, to this day, has retained its position as a leading force in Lithuanian cultural and nationality identity. The efforts by Catholic clergy to encourage religious awareness among the youth and the annoyance that this has engendered among the Communist leadership within the Lithuanian SSR have been reported. In November 1971, two Lithuanian priests were sentenced to one-year prison terms on charges of violating the law of separation of Church and state by teaching catechism to children.[28] Numerous petitions from Lithuanian Catholics, such as those sent to Leonid Brezhnev and UN Secretary General Kurt Waldheim in March 1972, in protest over the suppression of religious rights in Lithuania, underscore the continued importance that the Catholic Church retains as a religious center within the Republic.

Although it is difficult to distinguish between the purely religious and the cultural function which the Catholic Church serves in Lithuania, recreational programs of a non-religious type are undertaken by the Church as part of its contact with youth. There is word of a "priest in Lithuania who organized a sports club, and another who arranged an evening of dancing, a third who formed book-reading circles—all names and locations carefully noted and all projects having greater success than similar Party-planned activities."[29]

Church-affiliated youth programs were referred to in a recent issue of the Chronicle of the Lithuanian Catholic Church (samizdat). The Chronicle's discussion deals with a priest who "was sentenced because he violated Article 143 of the Penal Code of the Lithuanian SSR—He played volleyball with some children!" (Emphasis in the English translation.)[30]

The Lithuanian Communist party's concern that cultural and religious activities of the Church may become too popular among youth is at least partially explained by the resulting decrease in the appeal of the officially sponsored cultural activities. Although approached from an inverted position, the following remarks by the Director of the Division of Propaganda and Agitation in the Central Committee of the Lithuanian Communist Party indicate a correlation between an increase in Church appeal and a decline in the attractiveness of officially sanctioned activities:

Concrete observations show that a decrease in religiosity is accompanied in all areas by an increase in attendance at libraries, clubs, and movies, by a more active participation in independent artistic work (khudozhestvennaia samodeiatel'nost'), and in sports.[31]

A drive to curb competition from the Church no doubt explains the creation of such groups as the Vilnius City Club of Atheistic Thought, which exist on a Republic-wide basis, and, within a single year, delivers some 40,000 lectures on atheism.[32]

Curiously, Komsomol members are frequently supporters of the Catholic Church. One may explain this either on religious grounds or by the fact that, in many instances, officially sanctioned cultural programs are inadequate to satisfy the interests of youth, who, in turn, seek increasingly closer ties with the Church. The linkage between Lithuanian Komsomol members and the Church is shown by the example of Roman Kalanta, a young Lithuanian who immolated himself on May 14, 1972, in protest over Soviet suppression of nationality and religious rights:

> Kalanta was a member of the Communist Youth League
> and grew up in a family where all the brothers belonged
> to Communist youth organizations and the father to the
> Communist Party. At the same time it has been reported
> by travelers that young Kalanta was deeply religious des-
> pite his membership in the Communist Youth League,
> which requires commitment to atheism.[33]

Furthermore, a civil marriage ceremony in Lithuania is often followed by a religious ceremony. It is said that "the Communists are particularly incensed that this is being practiced by their own select youth in the Komsomol."[34]

Despite the seemingly important role played by the Catholic Church in Lithuanian religious and cultural life, religion is criticized only infrequently and in an oblique and cautious manner in Lithuania's Komsomol press. The allusions to religion which do appear, however, offer some insight into the tactics by which the Komsomol and Party leadership attempt to cope with the Church. For example, religion is referred to in a satirical poem, signed with a Russian name, attempting to ridicule religion as an entity made obsolete by the advent of the space age. In this poem, God is quoted as lamenting to himself: "I look wretched (ubogo) in the godless age of space ships."[35] Another reference to religion consists of a serialized story by a Russian journalist, recounting his experiences as a correspondent in the Ukraine during the Second World War. The story deals with the Uniate Church of the Ukraine, whose leaders are depicted as backward, venal, and superstitious.[36] Both these portrayals of religion are presented by writers with Russian names, something uncommon among the reporters for the Komsomol press of the Lithuanian SSR, virtually all of whom have Lithuanian names. Furthermore, no direct mention is made of the ills of the Catholic Church itself. Reference to the obsolescence of religion in the world of technology is a common atheistic theme, without specific relevance to the Lithuanian SSR. Likewise, the oblique reference to the religious life in the Ukraine some 30 years ago can hardly be interpreted as a virulent, polemical indictment of the Church in Lithuania in 1973. Such cautious treatment of religion reveals an unwillingness to provoke a recurrence of protest against Soviet policy toward religion in the Lithuanian SSR like those that erupted into violence in the spring of 1972.

Young people who reject the Komsomol and officially sponsored cultural activities also find an outlet in the establishment of a youth "counter-culture," many of whose characteristics are borrowed from the West. Unlike the Catholic Church of the Lithuanian SSR, which has an organizational structure, this sub-culture is largely amorphous. Frequent public criticism of what is termed the corruption of Lithuanian youth by Western dances and "music of the night clubs," suggests that the counter-culture raises a major challenge to institutionalized forms of cultural expression, and, by the same token, to the integrative pressures exerted by the Party and Komsomol leadership.[37] Often those condemning what they call the obvious influence of Western cultural patterns write as representatives of such institutions as the Ministry of Culture of the Lithuanian SSR. For example, an employee of the Scientific-Methodological Section of the Ministry of Culture decries the "anticultural" trends overtaking youth and urges support for efforts by governmental and Party agencies to issue rules of behavior to those attending dances.[38] Often such gatherings are described as a breeding ground for such anti-social behavior as "discourtesy, insolence, and dissoluteness."[39]

Apart from depicting Western dancing, long hair, and loud modern music as hostile toward ideological goals, these trends are occasionally berated as antithetical to the nationality culture of the Lithuanian SSR.[40] In a thoughtful appeal, "Fashion Passes On, Art Remains," one writer notes that knowing Western dances does not mean knowing the nationality dances of Lithuania.[41] Interestingly, here official attempts to counteract the youth subculture are pursued through the invocation of Lithuanian cultural distinctiveness and appeals to young people not to undermine this distinctiveness by copying alien trends. Such efforts at persuasion were answered by silence on the part of Lithuania's youth.

The attraction to Western trends may be an attempt on the part of the youth of the Lithuanian SSR to arrive at its own definition of cultural identity, following the rejection of the standard, officially sponsored ways of expression. As a striking example of this, one may cite a singer of Lithuanian nationality songs, lamenting the fact that his recitals before young audiences have been met with indifference and occasional laughter. He reflects woefully upon the lack of appreciation Lithuanian youth shows for "general culture" (obshchaia kul'tura).[42] Attempts to assert its uniqueness leads part of the Lithuanian youth to a total negation not only of the official ways of expressing cultural and nationality identity but also of the social norms. Thus, some young people engage in criminal, antisocial activities, including vandalism, defacing public property, uprooting trees, and smashing windows in new residential areas.[43] Here there is no constructive effort at creating an alternative channel for asserting nationality and self-identity; there is only a blunt rejection of the existing channels.

In conclusion, it is proposed that youth within the Lithuanian SSR constitute a major element for the expression of nationality consciousness and divisiveness. Such expression appears on two levels. First, one sees what may be termed "passive resistance" to the strong centripetal forces applied from the center, that is, the Komsomol, Party, and governmental authorities of the Lithuanian SSR. Dissected into its component parts, resistance emerges as an apathetic response to, and growing disengagement from, Komsomol and cultural activities which strive to impose a single Soviet national awareness and thereby to deprive Lithuanian youth of its distinctive nationality identity. "Disinvolvement" from centripetal forces, as it has been discussed here, has manifested itself in a variety of ways, most notably in a decline in attendance at integrative functions and in a lack of interest in the media through which those functions are promoted. On a second level, the expression of nationality consciousness and the attempts to counteract integrative pressures acquire a pronounced sense of activism, extending beyond passivity and indifference toward officially sponsored programs. Here we encounter an independent quest for alternative channels which will permit the youth of the Lithuanian SSR to develop its own perception of nationality identity.

The foregoing study supports the joint hypothesis of the group by pointing out the unique cultural position of the Lithuanian SSR as part of the Soviet West, by referring to integrative pressures found in the region, and by illustrating how one social group, the youth, has attempted to thwart those pressures and pursue its own course of nationality divisiveness. This study clearly demonstrates that some 30 years of Soviet rule in Lithuania have not impaired Lithuania's capacity for nationality assertiveness. As a reaction to integrative pressures, there has emerged a counterforce, which, in large measure, is shaped by the young and which is and will be decisive for Lithuania's continued nationality consciousness.

NOTES

1. "Naselenie nashei strany," Pravda, April 17, 1971, p. 3.
2. Ibid.
3. "Kazhdomu Komsomol'tsu-pechatnoe izdanie," Komsomol'-skaia pravda, November 15, 1972, p. 1
4. P. Al'ksnite, "Khoroshee nachalo mnogo znachit," Komsomol'-skaia pravda, January 6, 1973, p.1
5. "A chto dal'she," Komsomol'skaia pravda, January 14, 1973, p. 2.
6. G. Salis, "Kriticheskii signal: 30 iz 230-malo," Komsomol'-skaia pravda, February 7, 1973, p. 1.
7. "Luchshe raz uvidet', chem...," Komsomol'skaia pravda, February 7, 1973, p. 1.
8. L. Alekseiunas, "Ne poiaviatsia li 'bumazhnye' znachkisty?," Komsomol'skaia pravda, February 13, 1973, p. 4.
9. A. Ragaishis, "Na rotatore," Komsomol'skaia pravda, February 10, 1973, pp. 1-2.
10. Ibid.
12. Iu. Zhukas, "Kontserty studentov," Sovetskaia Litva, November 1, 1972, p. 4.
12. "Brat'ia v zhizni i poezii," Komsomol'skaia pravda, November 19, 1972, p. 4.
13. A. Vasinavskas, "Druzhba, druzhba," Komsomol'skaia pravda, November 16, 1972, p. 2.
14. "Daina i Doina," Komsomol'skaia pravda, November 12, 1972, p. 4.
15. B. Meshkauskas, "Na festival' v GDR," Sovetskaia Litva, November 7, 1972, p. 4.
16. K. Nainis, "Doubek-to viborne," Komsomol'skaia pravda, November 23, 1972, p. 2.
17. B. Meshkauskas, "Kontsertnaia afisha, noiabr' 1972 goda," Sovetskaia Litva, November 2, 1972, p. 4.
18. R. Noreikaite, "Konkurs molodykh akterov," Komsomol'skaia pravda, November 1, 1972, p. 4.
19. Iu. Potsius, "Nachalo puti," Komsomol'skaia pravda, December 3, 1972, p. 4.
20. "Pokazyvaiut budushchie khudozhniki," Komsomol'skaia pravda, November 12, 1972, p. 3.
21. P. Brazhenas, "Ispytanie debiutom," Komsomol'skaia pravda, February 11, 1973, p. 4.
22. "Brat'ia v zhizni i poezii," Komsomol'skaia pravda November 19, 1972, p. 4.
23. N. Steponkute, "Struitsia miagkii svet," Komsomol'skaia pravda, November 29, 1972, p. 4.

24. Iu. Zhukas, "Kontserty studentov," Sovetskaia Litva, November 1, 1972, p. 4.

25. I. Kunchinas, "Vecher poeticheskikh perevodov," Komsomol'-skaia pravda, November 29, 1972, p. 4.

26. J. Savasis, The War Against God in Lithuania (New York: Manyland Books, Inc., 1966), p. 13.

27. "Religious Persecution in Lithuania—Soviet Style," Lituanus Vol. 18 (Summer 1972), p. 56.

28. Ibid., pp. 52-53; also Chronicle of the Lithuanian Catholic Church, No. 1 (1972), pp. 11, 18.

29. Savasis, pp. 92-93. The reliability of this source is questionable, as the issue of Ogonek cited by Savasis contains no reference to church activity in the Lithuanian SSR. Efforts to establish the correct reference have proved unavailing.

30. Chronicle of the Catholic Church, No. 1 (1972), p. 46.

31. P. Mishutis, "Na nauchnoi osnove," Nauka i religiia, No. 3 (1972), p. 30.

32. Ibid., p. 32; also B. Iaunishkis, "Klub nauchnoi mysli," Komsomol'skaia pravda, November 28, 1972, p. 2.

33. Stanley Vardys, "Protests in Lithuania Not Isolated," Lituanus, Vol. 18 (Summer 1972), pp. 6-7.

34. Savasis, p. 123.

35. R. Kireev, "Bog i rakety," Komsomol'skaia pravda, February 22, 1973, p. 4.

36. Vladimir Beliaev, et al., "Kto tebia predal," Komsomol'-skaia pravda, February 1, 1973, pp. 1-4.

37. Cheslovas Norvaisha, "Eto zavisit ot menia, ot tebia, ot nas," Komsomol'skaia pravda, November 15, 1972, p. 2.

38. L. Ablenaite, "Kto kak umeet-tak i tantsuet?," Komsomol'-skaia pravda, November 18, 1972, p. 2.

39. G. Korsakene, "Vechnye chuvstva," Komsomol'skaia pravda, February 14, 1973, p. 4.

40. Beliaev, et al., "Eto zavisis ot menia, ot tebia ot nas," November 15, 1972, p. 2.

41. K. Poshkaitis, "Moda ukhodit, iskusstvo ostaetsia," Komsomol'skaia pravda, December 9, 1972, p. 2.

42. President kluba chitatelei, "Budem khoziaevami," Komsomol'skaia pravda, January 31, 1973, p. 4.

43. President kluba chitatelei, "Dolgo li terpet'," Komsomol' skaia pravda, January 7, 1973, p. 2.

10

MILITARY-PATRIOTIC
CAMPAIGNS IN ESTONIA
Claude Alexander

An important feature of the interaction between the opposing forces of nationality consciousness and homogenization-integration within the Soviet West is the sector devoted to preconscription military training and morale, an activity generally known as military-patriotic campaigns. Military-patriotic campaigns are Union-wide and involve both propaganda and organized training. Although the purpose of these endeavors is clearly integrative in nature, there are also elements of nationality consciousness evident in the themes and in the response of the populace to the activities. This paper focuses on military-patriotic campaigns in the Estonian SSR, an area which, because of its social, cultural, and economic characteristics, provides an excellent example of the role of integrative forces on the one hand, and the maintenance of nationality consciousness on the other.

Military-patriotic campaigns are regularly publicized in the Soviet Estonian press. A survey of Sovetskaia Estoniia, the Republic party and government organ, and Molodezh' Estonii, the Republic Komsomol newspaper during 1972-73, has shown that from over 80 articles on military-patriotic themes, about 60 percent make explicit or implicit references to the nationalities. The evidence utilized in this study is drawn from these two local press sources. The local press is the instrument of contact when the pressure for integration takes the form of propaganda. When training and education activities are employed, the press takes a secondary role as an instrument of inducement since the primary pressure for integration is transmitted through personal participation in activities.

In response to the development of more sophisticated forms of warfare, the Soviet military forces have become increasingly dependent upon highly technical and complex equipment, resulting in a growing need for technicians. At the same time, improved living standards and demands of the civilian economy for technical personnel has drawn capable individuals away from military life, which offers privileges and rewards but also harsh discipline and discomforts. This waning attraction of military service, together with shorter conscription periods, has created a problem of retaining skilled personnel on active duty. Military-patriotic campaigns are intended to provide a partial solution to this problem.[1]

The Estonian SSR and, to a lesser degree, the Soviet West in general, represent an acute form of this problem. Estonia has a highly industrialized and technologically advanced economy. Its population has an educational level well above the Soviet average. The Estonian living standard is far above the average of the USSR.[2] Therefore, potentially at least, Estonians are better able to satisfy the military demand for individuals with technical skills and aptitudes. Yet, with better living conditions than any other nationality, Estonians should be more strongly disinclined toward military service. This latter aversion is compounded by a recent separate political history and by a distinct cultural and linguistic identity.

Attracting Estonians to careers in the armed forces is an aspect of the integrative process. Integration means more than simply achieving the physical participation of Estonians in government activities. Since military service is assured by universal conscription, successful integration, in a more general sense, is contingent upon voluntary participation. Estonians must be induced to choose military service beyond the basic obligation, to contribute their technical skills fully, and to support government policies. These goals cannot be achieved solely by coercion. Homogenization, or a decrease in cultural differences, is not equivalent to integration but instead facilitates it. A good command of Russian improves military efficiency since Russian is the language of the Soviet Armed Forces. Further, homogenization reduces the possibilities for personal antagonisms in multiethnic units. Divisiveness, the opposite of integration, seldom takes the form of open opposition or of clearly expressed separatism in the Soviet context. Therefore, divisiveness appears only as subtle and indirect opposition in the form of reluctant participation, incomplete contribution of skills, or undermining government policies by inactivity. Apathy and indifference, especially as it affects young people, are subjects of integrative pressure. A distinct nationality identity is not the same as divisiveness but creates the conditions for the growth of it. Vitality may be regarded as the ability and tendency of a nationality to perpetuate its identity.

The interacting groups in military-patriotic campaigns may be divided roughly into government-related groups which apply pressure, and the nationality population which is the target. These two are not mutually exclusive, however, since an individual with strong divisive tendencies may be in the government and conversely, a supporter of Soviet policies and programs may not be.

The organizations participating in training and educational activities encompass a very large part of the population. Government groups that conduct the activities include the Dobrovol'noe Obshchestvo Sodeistviia Armii, Aviatsii i Flotu (Volunteer Society for the Assistance of the Army, Air Force, and Navy—abbreviated DOSAAF); the Komsomol; the Communist party; military, veteran and civil defense units; economic, labor and educational organizations; and sport and social groups.[3] Youth is the social stratum that receives the pressure from these activities, of course, but it may be argued that older generations are also influenced by these programs.

The fact that a large number and variety of organizations are involved in military-patriotic training and educational programs has several significant aspects. It implies that much broader objectives are intended than merely preparing young people for military service. Preconscription training could be more efficiently and effectively conducted by one or a few specialized organizations. The large number of groups involved instead suggests that a more general impact is to be achieved. The relationship of the activities to the military services and the militaristic nature of the programs permit greater influence of the Soviet armed forces over the participating groups. The constant, widespread attention given in the local press to these programs indicates that a high degree of importance is attached to the activities.

Military-patriotic training and educational programs are conducted in three phases: glorification, indoctrination and skill development. Glorification takes the form of meetings[4] or parades[5] in honor of World War II veterans, visits to the graves of fallen heroes[6] and memorials to military units and battles.[7] It serves to emphasize certain patterns of behavior and personality traits as being desirable. The glorified actions are service and loyalty to the USSR, heroic and selfless efforts in the military, and harmony and friendship among the nationalities.

The indoctrination phase is accomplished by meetings of young people with distinguished veterans and exemplary soldiers, by tours to memorials and places of glory, and by other methods of bringing young people into contact with examples or symbols of desirable behavior.[8] This indoctrination is a pressure on younger as well as older generations to emulate the patterns of social behavior and traits which are glorified or promoted by Soviet groups.

Skill development activities teach basic military skills and military-oriented forms of sport, and impart technical skills and aptitudes.[9] Difficulties in accomplishing these activities have been attributed mainly to a lack of qualified instructors and to the expense of necessary equipment, but also to indifference among the participating groups.

Some evidence of nationality identity and divisiveness have appeared through the reports on training and educational activities. Since 1964, Russian-language training for non-Russian ethnic groups has been assigned as a part of pre-draft preparation.[10] However, not a single word indicating the fulfillment of this program appeared in the Estonian press, a trend that seems to reflect a divisive attitude on the part of Estonians. Another example of nationality identity as manifested in military-patriotic propaganda has been the extensive publicity given to youth tours of World War II battlefields where Estonian soldiers fought on the Soviet side.[11]

While preconscription training is directed primarily at young people, military-patriotic propaganda is intended to influence a much broader audience. Newspaper staffs are the organizations most involved with press reports. However, the authors of propaganda accounts come from various backgrounds, such as professional military life, factory work, and Party membership.

Military-patriotic press accounts are typified by either historical or contemporary themes. They also may be categorized according to explicit or implicit references to or the absence of mention of nationalities.

Propaganda with historical themes concentrates on Soviet victories in World War II or on veterans and units of those battles. Articles that include no references to the nationalities serve to glorify the Soviet armed forces, the government, the Communist party and the entire Soviet society.[12] This strengthens the credibility and legitimacy of the government for the younger segments of the society. Such accounts glorify the older generations, whose qualities should increase the respect and admiration of young people for their leaders and their elders in general. These stories should also encourage older people to conform to the image portrayed by this evidence.

Historically-oriented reports making explicit mention of nationalities draw attention to examples of cooperation and solidarity of the various ethnic groups in the face of the German attack.[13] These allusions usually enumerate the multiethnic components of military units.

As in articles without reference to nationalities, accounts with explicit mention of them constantly reiterated clearly defined patterns of behavior: loyalty and self-sacrifice for the Soviet government, unity and harmony with other ethnic groups, and heroic military service. The frequent repetition of these themes and the similarity in content reduce the attractiveness of these accounts to a reading audience. It is likely, therefore, that their effectiveness is decreased.

One method used to improve the quality of the stories is to appeal to Estonian national identity. For example, in the case of a young Estonian partisan executed by the Germans, it is said: "[He] fought to the end for the Soviet Homeland side by side with his Russian and Belorussian brothers."[14] Thus, the message is clearly integrative; Estonians cooperated with Russians and other ethnic groups in defense of the USSR.

A more subtle approach to presenting the patterns of behavior described previously is found in historical military propaganda that makes references to the nationality question only by implication. Nationality may be openly stated or suggested by residence or by surname.[15] All of these stories are human interest accounts. The didactic messages are not given overtly but are demonstrated through the actions of the characters. The absence of blatantly repeated positions makes these accounts more readable and for this reason more effective.

Numerous articles have appeared about the Soviet Estonian Guards Infantry Corps of World War II.[16] These reports contain the same integrative pressures for loyalty to the Soviet government, cooperation with other ethnic groups, and participation in the Soviet armed forces. However, these stories more clearly articulate a theme of Estonian dependence on the rest of the Soviet Union during and after the war. The bonds of common suffering and mutual aid between Estonia and other republics of the USSR are also often stressed.

At the same time, strong suggestions of divisiveness and nationality identity arise in these articles. Publicity for an Estonian nationality military unit effectively maintains a distinct nationality history. Frequent mention of the Estonian character of famous military units begs the divisive question: Why are there no Estonian nationality formations in today's Soviet Army? Descriptions of outstanding performances by the Estonian Infantry Corps and its participation in the liberation of Estonia also seem to be thinly veiled assertions that Estonians function better in an ethnically homogeneous unit and that Estonia is capable of defending and preserving its own independence. Finally, participation in the Soviet Army against the Germans could easily be viewed as a marriage of necessity and not having direct relevance to the present era.

Military-patriotic propaganda on a current theme is directed more specifically at young people than is the historical approach. The current theme utilizes descriptions of young draftees and soldiers. Articles of this sort show exemplary traits, problem areas, and positive inducements to serve in the armed forces.

General traits defined for emulation by all young soldiers are military proficiency and attraction to hard work. Ambition for advancement and higher education, willingness to sacrifice personal interests for the good of the service, and imitation of elders in the patterns of behavior that are sanctioned by the government.[17] Certain

characteristics are singled out specifically for members of nationalities. Ethnic groups are commended for living and working together
harmoniously, and they must be especially loyal and vigilant in service to "the beloved Soviet Homeland."[18] Estonians and other nationalities in the armed forces have been called upon to explain the
status of their republic in the Soviet federation before mixed groups
of seniors and peers.[19] In this environment, particularly in the
Soviet military context, a non-Russian individual probably would not
speak negatively about Soviet treatment of nationalities. Thus, in an
outward manner at least, non-Russian soldiers are required to identify
themselves with the integral position of their nationality republic in
the USSR.

Estonians are described as having problems with the Russian
language in the service and as not having had sufficient preparation
for the military in pre-conscription training.[20] There have been
allusions to the idea that ethnic and cultural differences exacerbate
these deficiencies. The remedies which have been suggested for
Estonian soldiers are to work harder and to capitalize on their technical skills and the assistance available from other soldiers.

Only positive inducements have been described for performance
in the armed forces. These include material awards and prizes,
promotions, approval by peers and seniors, and publicity through
newspaper photos and articles.

In summary, propaganda with current and historical themes,
together with military-patriotic training and educational activities,
are methods used by the government to induce Estonians to accept
integration and homogenization into the larger Soviet society. In
order to achieve integration, certain patterns of behavior are suggested
for emulation. These patterns are loyalty to the Soviet Union, willing
participation in the armed forces, and friendship and cooperation
with other Soviet nationalities. Homogenization, which is important
to the achievement of integration, primarily takes the form of decreas-
ing language differences by spreading the use of Russian.

Expressions of Estonian nationality identity occur rather frequently in the local press in the forms of historical heritage and pride
of accomplishment. Nationality identity is also promoted by Soviet
groups in order to better achieve their own purposes.

Without a distinct Estonian identity, it would be difficult to
visualize any form of divisiveness. In the Soviet context, divisiveness
can only occur in a subtle or indirect manner. It usually takes the
form of apathetic performance in Soviet programs or indifference to
official policies. To a lesser degree, there are suggestions that
Estonia could maintain a more independent role relative to the USSR.
Of course, since the sources of data are government controlled newspapers, it is impossible to determine precisely the representative

attitudes of the Estonian population. It is clear that reluctance to learn Russian, to participate in preconscription military training, and perhaps to choose military careers are modes of nationality divisiveness.

The profile of the Estonian nationality is fragmented. Estonians vary in attitudes toward the Soviet government from strong support to acceptance out of necessity. No government groups have shown clear support for Estonian divisiveness although individuals in the government may take a more sympathetic approach. On the basis of the material surveyed, it is impossible to establish a trend of increasing divisiveness. The degree of integrative pressure being applied by Soviet groups and the lack of integration demonstrated by Estonians are indicative of a strong separate and dynamic nationality identity.

NOTES

1. Leon Goure, The Military Indoctrination of Soviet Youth (New York: National Strategy Information Center, 1973), pp. 12-13. In 1967, the length of mandatory military service was reduced by one year to two years for the Soviet Army, Air Force, and Border Guards, three years for the Navy, and only one year for individuals with advanced education. Simultaneously, the military draft was made universal. See: Drew Middleton, "Shortcomings in Training Worry Soviet Military Establishment," New York Times, March 19, 1973, p. 16.

2. Rein Taagepera, "Dissimilarities Among the Northwestern Soviet Republics," in Problems of Mini-Nations: Baltic Perspectives, ed. Arvids Ziedonis, et al. (San Jose, Calif.: Association for the Advancement of Baltic Studies, 1973).

3. "Mesiachnik oboronno-massovoi rabotu," Molodezh'Estonii, January 30, 1973, p. 1; I. Kasmerigi, "Chustvo loktia," Molodezh'-Estonii, January 26, 1973, p. 3; S. Vagin, "Antrakta ne budet," Sovetskaia Estoniia, January 10, 1973, p. 2.

4. "Praxdnovanie 28-i godovshchiny osvobozhdeniia Tallina ot fashistskikh zakhvatchikov," Sovetskaia Estoniia, September 24, 1972, p. 1; "Vstrecha voinov dvukh pokolenii," Molodezh'Estonii, December 1, 1972, p. 1.

5. "Tam, gde bylo razorvano kol'tso blokady," Molodezh'Estonii, January 19, 1973, p. 1.

6. Olev Eensalu, "Sviashchenna pamiat' geroev," Molodezh'-Estonii, January 1, 1973, p. 3; L. Rinne, "Po mestam boevoi slavy," Sovetskaia Estoniia, September 5, 1972, p. 3.

7. "Chastitsa armii bratsva i druzhba," Sovetskaia Estoniia, September 23, 1972, p. 1; "Krasnoe znamia-voinam," Sovetskaia Estoniia, January 25, 1973, p. 1.

8. S. Vagin, "Molodezh' prinimaet estafety," Sovetskaia Estoniia, September 19, 1972, p. 1; A. Allas, "Expeditsiia: moia rodina-SSSR," Molodezh' Estonii, January 30, 1973, p. 3.

9. "Puti ottsov-dorogi synovei," Sovetskaya Estoniia, September 24, 1972, p. 1.

10. "On Measures for the Further Improvement of Training of Pre-Draft and Draft Age Youths for Service in the Armed Forces of the USSR," KPSS o vooruzhennykh silakh Sovetskogo Soiuza, p. 371.

11. "Puti ottsov-dorogi synovei," p. 1.

12. A. Sovol'ev, "Slaven tvoi podvig, gorod-geroi Leningrad," Molodezh'Estonii, January 18, 1973, p. 2; M. Ushakov, "Gde ty, tovarishch michman?" Sovetskaia Estoniia, January 7, 1973, p. 2; Oleg Chechin, "Soldaty Ladogi," Sovetskaia Estoniia, January 11, 1973, p. 4.

13. Makan Dzhumagulov, "Krovnoe Bratsvo," Molodezh'Estonii, January 9, 1973, p. 2; Nikolai Churimov, "Mamaev Kurgan," Sovetskaia, Estoniia, January 25, 1973, p. 2.

14. N. Belov, "Za stroki 'Izveshcheniia'," Sovetskaia Estoniia, January 6, 1973, p. 4.

15. F. Kaur, "Dva soldaty," Sovetskaia Estoniia, September 23, 1972, p. 1; N. Malasai, "Sestry milocerdiia," Molodezh'Estonii, December 13, 1972; A. Tiupin, "I zagovorili 'katiushi'," Sovetskaia Estoniia, January 18, 1973, p. 2.

16. "Prazdnovanie 28-i godovshchiny. . ."; A. Pankseev, "V internatsional—nom stroiu," Kommunist Estonii, No. 9 (September 1972), pp. 40-48.

17. G. Verkhoturov, "Nuzhen individual'nyi podkhod," Molodezh' Estonii, January 10, 1973, p. 2; S. Nemtsev, "Raketnyi grom," and V. Kuznetsov, "Smelye liudi," Molodezh' Estonii, January 24, 1973, p p. 2; I. Gaspl', "Vpered," Sovetskaia Estoniia, September 10, 1972, p. 1.

18. I. Beliaev, "Sluzhu Sovetskomu Soiuzu," Molodezh'Estonii, January 24, 1973, p. 2.

19. Ibid.

20. A. Tatsienko, "Ratnais doublest'," Molodezh'Estonii, January 24, 1973, p. 2; L. Firsov, "Zdes', naxastave geroia," Molodezh' Estonii, January 26, 1973, p. 2.

POPULATION OF MAJOR ETHNIC GROUPS
IN REPUBLICS OF THE SOVIET WEST,
1959 AND 1970

Ethnic Groups	Population		Percentage of Total	
	1959	1970	1959	1970
Ukrainian SSR	41,869,046	47,126,517		
Ukrainians	32,158,493	35,283,857	76.8	74.9
Russians	7,090,813	9,126,331	16.9	19.4
Jews	840,311	777,126	2.0	1.6
Belorussians	290,890	385,847	.7	.8
Poles	363,297	295,107	.9	.6
Moldavians	241,650	265,902	.6	.6
Bulgarians	219,409	234,390	.5	.5
Others	664,183	757,957	1.6	1.6
Belorussian SSR	8,055,714	9,002,338		
Belorussians	6,532,035	7,289,610	81.1	81.0
Russians	660,159	938,161	8.2	10.4
Poles	538,881	382,600	6.7	4.3
Ukrainians	133,061	190,839	1.7	2.1
Jews	150,084	148,011	1.9	1.6
Others	41,494	53,117	.4	.6
Lithuanian SSR	2,711,445	3,128,236		
Lithuanians	2,150,767	2,506,751	79.3	80.1
Russians	231,014	267,989	8.5	8.6
Poles	230,107	240,203	8.5	7.7
Belorussians	30,256	45,412	1.1	1.5
Ukrainians	17,692	25,099	.7	.8
Jews	24,672	23,564	.9	.8
Others	26,937	19,218	1.0	.5
Moldavian SSR	2,884,477	3,568,873		
Moldavians	1,886,566	2,303,916	65.4	64.6
Ukrainians	420,820	506,560	14.6	14.2
Russians	292,930	414,444	10.2	11.6
Gagauz	95,856	124,902	3.3	3.5
Jews	95,107	98,072	2.1	2.7
Bulgarians	61,652	73,776	2.1	2.1
Others	31,546	47,203	1.1	1.3

Ethnic Groups	Population		Percentage of Total	
	1959	1970	1959	1970
Latvian SSR	2,093,458	2,364,127		
Latvians	1,297,881	1,341,805	62.0	56.8
Russians	556,448	704,599	26.6	29.8
Belorussians	61,587	94,898	2.9	4.0
Poles	59,774	63,045	2.9	2.7
Ukrainians	29,440	53,461	1.4	2.3
Lithuanians	32,383	40,589	1.5	1.7
Jews	36,592	36,680	1.7	1.6
Others	19,353	29,050	1.0	1.1
Estonian SSR	1,196,791	1,356,079		
Estonians	892,653	925,157	74.6	68.2
Russians	240,227	334,620	20.1	24.7
Ukrainians	15,769	28,086	1.3	2.1
Belorussians	10,930	18,732	.9	1.4
Finns	16,699	18,537	1.4	1.4
Jews	5,436	5,288	.5	.4
Others	15,077	25,659	1.2	1.8
Soviet West	58,810,931	66,546,170		
Ukrainians	32,775,275	36,087,902	55.7	54.2
Russians	9,071,591	11,786,144	15.4	17.7
Belorussians	6,925,698	7,844,826	11.8	11.8
Moldavians	2,128,216	2,571,618	3.6	3.9
Lithuanians	2,202,035	2,568,503	3.7	3.9
Latvians	1,316,637	1,360,235	2.2	2.0
Jews	1,152,202	1,088,741	2.0	1.6
Estonians	901,444	934,062	1.5	1.4
Poles	1,132,285	988,505	1.9	1.5

Sources: Itogi vsesoiuznoi perepisi naseleniia 1959 goda
(Moscow: Gosstatizdat, 1962-63); Itogi vsesoiuznoi perepisi naseleniia
1970 goda (Moscow: Statistika, 1973), IV.

SELECTED SOCIOECONOMIC CHARACTERISTICS
OF REPUBLICS OF THE SOVIET WEST, 1970

Unit	Percent Urban[a]	Percent Secondary Education[b]	Crude Birth Rate per 1000	Crude Death Rate per 1000
Ukrainian SSR	55	49.4	15.2	8.9
Belorussian SSR	43	44.0	16.2	7.6
Lithuanian SSR	50	38.2	17.6	8.9
Moldavian SSR	32	39.7	19.4	7.4
Latvian SSR	62	51.7	14.5	11.2
Estonian SSR	65	50.6	15.8	11.1
USSR	56	48.3	17.4	8.2

[a]Census definition of "urban."
[b]The percentage of the population aged ten years or more having higher and secondary (middle) education, including incomplete secondary.

Source: Narodnoe khoziaistvo SSSR v 1970 g. (Moscow: Statistika, 1971), pp. 10-11, 25, 50-51.

SELECTED BIBLIOGRAPHY

The following are selected books and articles, in English, concerning the republics of the Soviet West and the titular nationalities thereof. The list is not exhaustive; an attempt has been made to limit the selections to more recent works.

BELORUSSIA

Lubachko, Ivan S. Belorussia Under Soviet Rule. Lexington: University Press of Kentucky, 1972.

Pipes, Richard. The Formation of the Soviet Union. rev. ed. New York: Atheneum, 1968. Pages 9-12, 73-75, 150-154.

Shabad, Theodore. Basic Industrial Resources of the U.S.S.R. New York: Columbia University Press, 1969. Pages 201-206.

Vakar, Nicholas P. Belorussia: The Making of a Nation. Cambridge, Mass.: Harvard University Press, 1956.

_____. "The Belorussian People Between Nationhood and Extinction." Ethnic Minorities in the Soviet Union. Ed. Erich Goldhagen. New York: Praeger, 1968. Pages 218-228.

THE BALTIC REPUBLICS

Dunn, Stephen P. Cultural Processes In the Baltic Area Under Soviet Rule. Research Series No. 11, Institute of International Studies, University of California, Berkeley, 1966.

Pennar, Jaan. "Nationalism in the Soviet Baltics." Ethnic Minorities in the Soviet Union. Ed. Erich Goldhagen. New York: Praeger, 1968. Pages 198-217.

Shabad, Pages 207-213.

Taagepera, Rein. "Dissimilarities Between the Northwestern Soviet Republics." Problems of Mini-Nations: Baltic Perspectives. Ed. A. Ziedonis, R. Taagepera, M. Valgemae. San Jose, Calif.: Association for the Advancement of Baltic Studies, 1973.

Vardys, V. Stanley. Lithuania Under the Soviets. New York: Praeger, 1965.

THE UKRAINE

Armstrong, John A. Ukrainian Nationalism. New York: Columbia
University Press, 1963.

Bilinsky, Yaroslav. The Second Soviet Republic: The Ukraine After
World War II. New Brunswick: Rutgers University Press,
1964.

_____. "Assimilation and Ethnic Assertiveness Among Ukrainians
of the Soviet Union." Ethnic Minorities in the Soviet Union.
Ed. Erich Goldhagen. New York: Praeger, 1968. Pages 147-
184.

Dzyuba, Ivan. Internationalism or Russification? 2nd Ed. London:
Weidenfeld and Nicolson, 1968.

Lydoplh, Paul E. Geography of the U.S.S.R. 2nd Ed. New York:
Wiley, 1970. Pages 90-119.

Manning, Clarence A. Twentieth Century Ukraine. New York: Book-
man, 1951.

Pipes, Pages 9-11, 114-150.

Shabad, Pages 173-199.

Sullivant, Robert S. Soviet Politics and the Ukraine, 1917-1957.
New York: Columbia University Press, 1962.

MOLDAVIA

Lydolph, Pages 119-122.

Moseley, Philip E. "Is Bessarabia Next?" Foreign Affairs, Vol. 18,
No. 3 (1940).

RALPH S. CLEM, Ph.D. in Geography, Columbia University, is Assistant Professor of International Relations, Florida International University, Miami. Among his publications is: "The Impact of Demographic and Socioeconomic Forces Upon the Nationality Question in Central Asia," in Edward Allworth, ed., The Nationality Question in Soviet Central Asia (Praeger, 1973).

CLAUDE ALEXANDER, M.I.A., Columbia University, and Certificate of the Russian Institute, Columbia University, is currently Legislative Assistant to Senator Robert Dole of Kansas.

BRIAN CONNELLY, M.I.A., Columbia University, is in the publishing field. He is a former editor of the Journal of International Affairs; of particular interest to readers of this book is Volume 27, No. 1 (1973), an issue devoted to "Political Integration in Multinational States."

NICHOLAS DIMA, M.Ph., Columbia University, is currently a Ph.D. candidate in the Department of Geography, Columbia University.

WALTER FELDMAN, M.A. in Middle East Languages and Cultures, Columbia University, is working for an advanced degree at Columbia University.

EMMETT GEORGE, M.I.A., Columbia University, is now a general assignment reporter for the Chicago Tribune.

MARY ANN GROSSMAN, M.I.A., Columbia University, and Certificate of the Russian Institute, Columbia University, is currently on the staff of the Council on International Educational Exchange.

NORMAN KASS, M.I.A., Columbia University, Certificate of the Russian Institute, Columbia University, and M.A., University of Pennsylvania, now works for a major New York bank.

JOAN T. WEINGARD, M.A. in Uralic Studies, Columbia University, is a Ph.D. candidate in Uralic Studies at Columbia.

DEVELOPMENT REGIONS IN THE SOVIET
UNION AND EASTERN EUROPE
          edited by Andrew F. Burghardt

THE NATIONALITY QUESTION IN SOVIET
CENTRAL ASIA
          edited by Edward Allworth

SOVIET ASIA—BIBLIOGRAPHIES: The Iranian,
Mongolian, and Turkic Nationalities
          edited by Edward Allworth

THE SOVIET ECONOMY IN REGIONAL
PERSPECTIVE
               edited by V. N. Bandera
               and Z. L. Melnyk

THE SOVIET TREATMENT OF JEWS
          Harry G. Shaffer